The Pae
Authentic Recipes for the Classic Spanish Dish

Heel veel plezier met het maken van de verschillende paella's

Savor Supper Society Cafe Tao

Eet smakelijk
Arnold en Hanneke ♡

Copyright © 2023 Savor Supper Society Cafe Tao
All rights reserved.
:

Contents

INTRODUCTION 7

1. Classic Valencian Paella 9
2. Seafood Paella 9
3. Chicken and Chorizo Paella 10
4. Vegetarian Paella 12
5. Mixed Paella (Seafood and Meat) 13
6. Black Paella (Paella Negra) 14
7. Mushroom Paella 15
8. Shrimp and Saffron Paella 16
9. Squid Ink Paella 17
10. Lobster Paella 18
11. Paella with Artichokes and Peas 19
12. Paella with Green Beans and Asparagus 20
13. Duck and Mushroom Paella 21
14. Paella with Roasted Red Peppers 22
15. Paella with Clams and Mussels 23
16. Paella with Pork Ribs and Beans 25
17. Paella with Rabbit and Snails 26
18. Paella with Octopus and Squid 27
19. Paella with Chicken and Shrimp 28
20. Paella with Lamb and Rosemary 29
21. Paella with Spinach and Feta 30
22. Paella with Chorizo and Prawns 31
23. Paella with Calamari and Green Olives 32
24. Paella with Salmon and Peppers 33
25. Paella with Beef and Peas 34
26. Paella with Zucchini and Eggplant 35
27. Paella with Scallops and Bacon 36

28. Paella with Cod and White Beans 37
29. Paella with Pork Tenderloin and Chorizo 38
30. Paella with Green Peppers and Tomatoes 39
31. Paella with Anchovies and Capers 41
32. Paella with Shrimp and Chorizo 42
33. Paella with Crab and Tomato 43
34. Paella with Chicken and Sausage 44
35. Paella with Baby Squid and Piquillo Peppers 45
36. Paella with Sardines and Lemon 46
37. Paella with Veal and Artichokes 47
38. Paella with Green Peas and Mint 48
39. Paella with Duck and Figs 49
40. Paella with Swordfish and Olives 50
41. Paella with Rabbit and Chickpeas 51
42. Paella with Shrimp and Green Beans 52
43. Paella with Lamb and Eggplant 53
44. Paella with Clams and Chorizo 54
45. Paella with Pork and Pineapple 55
46. Paella with Squid and Peas 56
47. Paella with Chicken and Peppers 57
48. Paella with Beef and Mushrooms 58
49. Paella with Asparagus and Pesto 59
50. Paella with Lobster and Tomatoes 60
51. Paella with Sausage and Peppers 61
52. Paella with Cod and Chickpeas 62
53. Paella with Pork and Cauliflower 63
54. Paella with Shrimp and Asparagus 64
55. Paella with Chicken and Green Olives 65
56. Paella with Lamb and Mint 67

57. Paella with Spinach and Chickpeas 68

58. Paella with Clams and Spinach 69

59. Paella with Duck and Orange 70

60. Paella with Swordfish and Peppers 71

61. Paella with Rabbit and Green Beans 72

62. Paella with Crab and Corn 73

63. Paella with Chicken and Leeks 74

64. Paella with Veal and Mushrooms 75

65. Paella with Green Peas and Sausage 76

66. Paella with Shrimp and Zucchini 77

67. Paella with Lamb and Caramelized Onions 78

68. Paella with Clams and Piquillo Peppers 79

69. Paella with Pork and Apples 80

70. Paella with Squid and Tomatoes 81

71. Paella with Chicken and Mushrooms 82

72. Paella with Beef and Green Beans 83

73. Paella with Asparagus and Sun-Dried Tomatoes 84

74. Paella with Lobster and Corn 85

75. Paella with Sausage and Eggplant 86

76. Paella with Cod and Potatoes 87

77. Paella with Pork and Red Peppers 89

78. Paella with Shrimp and Spinach 90

79. Paella with Chicken and Piquillo Peppers 91

80. Paella with Lamb and Garlic 92

81. Paella with Green Peas and Bacon 93

82. Paella with Clams and Bell Peppers 94

83. Paella with Duck and Mushrooms 95

84. Paella with Swordfish and Zucchini 96

85. Paella with Rabbit and Bell Peppers 97

86. Paella with Shrimp and Bell Peppers 98

87. Paella with Crab and Bell Peppers 99

88. Paella with Chicken and Bell Peppers 100

89. Paella with Lamb and Bell Peppers 101

90. Paella with Green Peas and Shrimp 102

91. Paella with Clams and Chicken 103

92. Paella with Pork and Bell Peppers 104

93. Paella with Squid and Bell Peppers 105

94. Paella with Beef and Bell Peppers 106

95. Paella with Asparagus and Shrimp 107

96. Paella with Lobster and Shrimp 108

97. Paella with Sausage and Shrimp 109

98. Paella with Cod and Shrimp 111

99. Paella with Pork and Shrimp 112

CONCLUSION 114

INTRODUCTION

This cookbook, "The Paella Master: 99 Authentic Recipes for the Classic Spanish Dish", is a repository of international flavors. It encompasses a wide variety of recipes that bring the taste of Spain to everyone's dinner table. From beginner cooks to experienced aficionados, there is something here for everyone. The book contains 99 different recipes for every kind and style of paella, ranging from traditional to inventive. Each of these recipes is authentic Spanish cuisine from regions all over the country.

The Paella Master contains detailed instructions on what to do and what to look out for when preparing and serving the classic for a meal. Whether you are using long-grain rice, saffron threads, or other traditional ingredients, the cookbook will guide you through it step by step. The book also includes information on helpful kitchen tools, such as large pans, wooden spoons, and different cooking methods.

The recipes included in The Paella Master range from the simple to the challenging. From the classic Valencian Paella to the Andalusian Seafood Paella, you are sure to find something to satisfy your appetite. Whether you want to recreate traditional paellas or experiment with new combinations of ingredients, this is the cookbook for you. The Paella Master also provides guidance on what accompaniments go best with each dish.

In addition to the recipes, The Paella Master provides information on the history and culture of this classic dish. Readers are given an in-depth look into why paella is so popular, and how it has evolved throughout the years. People are encouraged to experiment and add their own spin to the traditional paella dishes.

The Paella Master is the perfect tool for anyone looking to recreate the taste and texture of Spain in their own kitchen. Whether you are an experienced chef or a beginner cook, there is something here for everyone. With delicious flavors and interesting ingredients, you won't be disappointed. This book will provide you with all the tools you need to start making your own paellas.

1. Classic Valencian Paella

This classic Valencian Paella is a must-try for all lovers of Spanish food. Perfectly cooked with delicious saffron rice, combined with vegetables, beans, and your choice of meat or seafood, this wonderful dish is sure to be a family favorite. Serving: 4-6 Preparation time: 15 minutes Ready time: 45 minutes

Ingredients:
• 1 tablespoon olive oil • 1 onion, finely chopped • 2 cloves garlic, finely chopped • 1 teaspoon paprika • 2 cups short-grain paella rice • 2 cups hot fish or vegetable stock • 4 Roma tomatoes, chopped • 1/2 teaspoon saffron threads • 1 large red bell pepper, seeded and cut into small strips • 1 cup peas • 4 ounces pimiento-stuffed olives • 2 cups cooked lobster, crab, shrimp, chicken, or pork (optional) • 1/2 teaspoon freshly ground black pepper

Instructions:
1. Heat olive oil in a large pan over medium heat. Add the onion and garlic and cook until the onion is softened, about 5 minutes.
2. Stir in the paprika and rice, cook for 1-2 minutes.
3. Add the stock, tomatoes, saffron, and red bell pepper. Simmer over medium low heat, stirring occasionally, for 15 minutes.
4. Add the peas, olives, and your choice of meat or seafood. Simmer for an additional 15 minutes.
5. Season with black pepper, and remove from heat. Let rest for 10 minutes before serving.

Nutrition information: Serving size: 6 | Calories: 315 kcal | Fat: 8 g | Carbohydrates: 40 g | Protein: 15 g

2. Seafood Paella

Seafood Paella is a popular Spanish dish consisting of seafood, rice, vegetables, herbs, and spices. It's flavorful and surprisingly easy to make.
Serving: 6
Preparation time: 10 minutes

Ready time: 35 minutes

Ingredients:
- 1/2 cup olive oil
- 3 garlic cloves, minced
- 1 onion, chopped
- 2 cups Spanish bomba or Calasparra rice
- 4 cups fish stock or vegetable stock
- 1 red bell pepper, chopped
- 1 teaspoon smoked paprika
- 1 teaspoon saffron threads
- 1 teaspoon oregano
- Salt and pepper, to taste
- 1/2 pound shrimp, peeled and deveined
- 1/2 pound clams, cleaned
- 1/2 pound mussels, cleaned

Instructions:
1. Heat the olive oil in a large skillet or paella pan over medium-high heat. Add the garlic and onion and cook for 2-3 minutes.
2. Add the rice, stock, bell pepper, paprika, saffron, oregano, salt, and pepper and stir everything together.
3. Reduce the heat to low, cover the pan, and allow the mixture to simmer for 15-20 minutes.
4. Uncover the pan and add the shrimp, clams, and mussels. Stir everything together.
5. Cover the pan and cook for an additional 10-15 minutes, or until the rice is tender and the seafood is cooked through.
6. Serve hot and enjoy!

Nutrition information:
Calories: 463 kcal, Protein: 23g, Total Fat: 25g, Sodium: 1380mg, Saturated Fat: 4g, Potassium: 345mg, Carbohydrates: 33g, Fiber: 2g, Sugar: 2g, Vitamin A: 745 IU, Vitamin C: 41.3mg, Calcium: 116mg, Iron: 2.4mg

3. Chicken and Chorizo Paella

Chicken and Chorizo Paella is a delightful Spanish-style rice dish that combines tender chicken and smoky chorizo with saffron-infused broth and plenty of fresh vegetables. This version is cooked in a skillet, making it easy to prepare in no time.

Serving: 8
Preparation time: 15 minutes
Ready time: 40 minutes

Ingredients:
- 2 tablespoons olive oil
- 2 cloves garlic, minced
- 1 red bell pepper, chopped
- 1 onion, chopped
- 8 ounces chorizo, diced
- 2 teaspoons smoked paprika
- 1/2 teaspoon each salt and pepper
- 4 skinless, boneless chicken thighs, cut into 1-inch pieces
- 1 1/2 cups Arborio rice
- 1/2 teaspoon saffron threads
- 3 1/2 cups low-sodium chicken broth
- 2 plum tomatoes, diced
- 1/2 cup frozen peas
- 2 tablespoons chopped fresh parsley

Instructions:
1. Heat the oil in a large non-stick skillet or Dutch ovenover medium-high heat. Add the garlic, pepper, and onion and cook, stirring often, until the vegetables are softened, about 5 minutes.
2. Add the chorizo and season with the paprika, salt, and pepper, stirring often to break up the sausage into small pieces. Continue cooking until the sausage is lightly browned, about 3 minutes.
3. Add the chicken and cook until lightly browned, about 5 minutes.
4. Add the rice and stir to combine. Add the saffron and broth and bring to a boil. Reduce the heat to low, cover, and simmer for 15 minutes.
5. Add the tomatoes and peas and cook, uncovered, until the rice is tender and the liquid is absorbed, about 10 minutes.
6. Sprinkle with parsley and serve.

Nutrition information:

Calories: 350, Fat: 17g, Saturated fat: 5g, Carbohydrates: 26g, Protein: 22g, Sodium: 846mg, Fiber: 3g, Cholesterol: 79mg

4. Vegetarian Paella

Vegetarian Paella is a Spanish-style rice dish with plenty of veggies that can be enjoyed by vegetarians and meat-eaters alike!
Serving: Serves 6
Preparation Time: 10 minutes
Ready Time: 35 minutes

Ingredients:
-3 tablespoons olive oil
-1 onion, diced
-2 cloves garlic, minced
-1 red pepper, diced
-1 teaspoon smoked paprika
-1/2 teaspoon dried oregano
-2 cups short-grain paella rice
-4 cups vegetable stock
-1 (14.5-ounce) can fire roasted diced tomatoes
-1/2 cup frozen peas
-1/2 cup frozen corn
-1 lemon, wedges

Instructions:
1. Heat the olive oil in a large skillet or paella pan over medium heat. Add the onion, garlic, and red pepper and cook for 5 minutes.
2. Add the smoked paprika and dried oregano and cook for 1 minute more.
3. Add the paella rice and cook for 2 minutes, stirring constantly.
4. Pour in the vegetable stock and canned tomatoes. Bring to a boil, reduce heat to low and simmer for 15 minutes, stirring occasionally.
5. Add the frozen peas and frozen corn and continue to simmer for 10 minutes more, until the rice is tender.
6. Squeeze a few lemon wedges over the top before serving.

Nutrition information: Calories: 270, Fat: 6g, Carbohydrates: 48g, Protein: 5g, Sodium: 472mg, Fiber: 4g

5. Mixed Paella (Seafood and Meat)

Mixed Paella is a delicious and traditional Spanish dish with a variety of flavors from the combination of different proteins. It combines elements from seafood and meets to create a delicious, unique, and filling meal.
Servings: 4
Preparation time: 20 minutes
Ready time: 60 minutes

Ingredients:
- 1 tablespoon extra virgin olive oil
- 1 onion, diced
- 2 cups long grain rice
- 4 cloves garlic, minced
- 4 cups vegetable broth
- 1 cup frozen peas
- 1 teaspoon smoked paprika
- ½ teaspoon saffron
- ½ teaspoon cumin
- ½ teaspoon cayenne pepper
- Salt to taste
- 1 teaspoon lemon zest
- 8 ounces chorizo, diced
- 12 ounces shrimp, peeled and deveined
- 4 ounces mussels, cleaned
- 8 ounces calamari, cut into rings

Instructions:
1. Heat olive oil in a large pot over medium heat. Add the onion and sauté until softened, about 5 minutes.
2. Add the rice, garlic, vegetable broth, peas, paprika, saffron, cumin, cayenne pepper, and salt to taste. Stir to combine. Bring the mixture to a boil, reduce heat to low, and simmer for 25 minutes until the rice is cooked and the liquid is absorbed.

3. Add the lemon zest, chorizo, shrimp, mussels, and calamari. Stir to combine and simmer for an additional 10 minutes until the seafood is cooked through.

Nutrition information:
Calories: 457 kcal, Carbohydrates: 58 g, Protein: 22 g, Total Fat: 15 g, Cholesterol: 177 mg, Sodium: 1266 mg, Fiber: 4 g, Sugar: 3 g

6. Black Paella (Paella Negra)

Black Paella, or Paella Negra, is a seafood dish originating in Valencia. It has a dark color due to the squid ink and distinct flavor that goes perfectly with the meat and vegetable combination.
Serving: 6
Preparation Time: 15-20 minutes
Ready Time: 45 minutes

Ingredients:
- 4 cups chicken broth
- 1 teaspoon saffron threads
- 1/4 cup olive oil
- 1/2 teaspoon salt
- 1 teaspoon black pepper
- 1 onion, chopped
- 2 garlic cloves, minced
- 1 red pepper, chopped
- 2 cups Bombay Bomba or Valencia Calasparra Rice
- 1/2 cup dry white wine
- 400 grams squid, cleaned and cut into rings
- 250 grams shrimp
- 250 grams mussels, cleaned
- 4 tablespoons squid ink

Instructions:
1. Heat the chicken broth in a large pot, and add the saffron.
2. In a separate pan, heat the olive oil. Add the salt, pepper, onion, garlic, and red pepper. Cook until the onion and pepper are soft.
3. Add the rice to the pan and stir until coated in the oil.

4. Add the white wine and bring to a boil. Simmer for 5-10 minutes, or until the rice has absorbed most of the liquid.
5. Add the cooked vegetables to the pot of broth. Stir in the squid, shrimp, mussels, and squid ink.
6. Simmer over low heat for 25-30 minutes, or until the broth and rice are completely cooked.

Nutrition information: per serving, calories 390, protein 29g, carbohydrates 44g, fat 11g

7. Mushroom Paella

This classic Spanish dish is an easy and delicious way to feed a crowd! Mushroom Paella is an impressive yet simple recipe that is sure to be a hit at any dinner table.
Serving: Serves 4 to 6
Preparation Time: 10 minutes
Ready Time: 25 minutes

Ingredients:
- 2 tablespoons olive oil
- 2 cloves garlic, chopped
- 1 onion, chopped
- 3 cups Crimini mushrooms, sliced
- 2 tablespoons smoked paprika
- 2 cups long-grain white rice
- 4 cups vegetable stock
- 10 ounces jarred roasted red peppers, chopped
- 2 tablespoons fresh parsley for garnish
- Salt and black pepper, to taste

Instructions:
1. Heat olive oil in a large skillet over medium heat. Add garlic and onion and cook, stirring often, until softened, about 5 minutes.
2. Add mushrooms, smoked paprika, and a pinch of salt and pepper; cook for 5 minutes more.

3. Add the rice and stir to combine. Pour in the vegetable stock, stir to combine, and bring to a boil. Reduce heat to a simmer and cook for 15 minutes, stirring occasionally.
4. Add the roasted red peppers and season with salt and pepper, to taste. Cook for 5 minutes more.
5. Garnish with parsley and serve.

Nutrition information: Per serving: 194 calories, 2g fat, 33g carbohydrates, and 6g protein.

8. Shrimp and Saffron Paella

Shrimp and Saffron Paella is a delicious Spanish dish, combining saffron rice and shrimp. It is both flavorful and vibrant, and is the perfect center piece for any dinner gathering or special occasion.
Serving: 8 servings
Preparation Time: 15 minutes
Ready Time: 45 minutes

Ingredients:
- 2 tablespoons olive oil
- 1 onion, diced
- 2 garlic cloves, minced
- 1 teaspoon smoked paprika
- 1 red pepper, diced
- 2 cups paella or Arborio rice
- 4 cups chicken or vegetable stock
- 1 pinch of saffron
- 1/2 teaspoon sea salt
- 1/2 teaspoon freshly ground black pepper
- 1/2 teaspoon dried oregano
- 2-3 tomatoes, diced
- 1/2 cup frozen peas
- 1 pound large shrimp, peeled and deveined
- 1 small lemon, cut into wedges

Instructions:

1. Heat the olive oil in large skillet over medium-high heat and add the onions, garlic, paprika and red pepper. Sauté until the vegetables are lightly golden, about 5 minutes.
2. Add the rice to the skillet and stir to coat in the oil and vegetables.
3. Pour in the chicken stock, season with the saffron, salt, pepper, oregano, stirring to combine.
4. Bring the mixture to a simmer, then reduce the heat to low and cover. Simmer for 20 minutes, stirring occasionally.
5. After 20 minutes, stir in the diced tomatoes, peas and shrimp and cook for an additional 10 minutes, or until the rice is cooked and the shrimp is cooked through.
6. Serve the paella with lemon wedges.

Nutrition information: per serving; Calories 308, Total Fat 8 g, Sodium 422g, Carbohydrates 37 g, Protein 18 g, Fiber 3 g

9. Squid Ink Paella

A classic and beautiful Spanish dish, Squid Ink Paella is a delicious seafood dish featuring fried squid and saffron rice with a tinge of dark color from squid ink.
Serving: 4-6
Preparation time: 45 minutes
Ready time: 1 hour 15 minutes

Ingredients:
-2 tablespoons extra-virgin olive oil
-1 medium onion, thinly sliced
-2 cloves garlic, minced
-2 teaspoons paprika
-1/2 teaspoon saffron
-1/2 teaspoon freshly ground pepper
-3 cups short-grain paella rice
-5 cups fish stock
-1 tablespoon squid ink
-2 teaspoons salt
-1 pound squid, cleaned and cut into rings
-1/2 pound peeled shrimp

-1/2 pound fresh mussels
-1/2 cup fresh parsley, chopped

Instructions:
1. Heat the oil in a large paella pan or wide skillet over medium heat.
2. Add the onion and garlic and cook, stirring often, until softened, about 8 minutes.
3. Add the paprika, saffron, pepper and rice and cook, stirring constantly, for 2 minutes.
4. Add the stock, squid ink and salt and bring to a boil. Lower the heat to a simmer and cook, uncovered, for 15 minutes.
5. Add the squid, shrimp and mussels and cook, stirring occasionally, until the seafood is cooked through, about 10 minutes.
6. Stir in the parsley and serve.

Nutrition information: Per Serving: 370 calories; 10 g of fat; 28 g of carbohydrates; 37 g of protein; 3 g of fiber.

10. Lobster Paella

Lobster Paella is a traditional Spanish dish that combines the flavors of lobster, vegetables, and rice for a delicious and flavorful meal. Serve this with a light salad and a glass of white wine for a complete meal.
Serving: Serves 4-6
Preparation time: 10 minutes
Ready time: 55 minutes

Ingredients:
- 1 shallot, finely chopped
- 4 cloves garlic, finely minced
- 2 tablespoons olive oil
- 2 cups Arborio rice
- 2 cups chicken stock
- 2 cups water
- 2 cups frozen peas
- 2 (8-ounce) tails cooked lobster, chopped
- 1 teaspoon paprika
- 2 tablespoons parsley, finely chopped

- Juice of 1 lemon
- Salt, to taste
- Freshly ground black pepper

Instructions:
1. In a large, non-stick skillet over medium heat, sauté the shallot and garlic in olive oil until the shallot is translucent.
2. Add the rice and stirring constantly, cook until the rice is lightly toasted (about 5 minutes).
3. Add both the chicken stock and water and bring to a boil.
4. Reduce the heat to low and simmer until the liquid is nearly absorbed (about 20 minutes).
5. Add the peas, lobster, paprika, parsley, and lemon juice and stir to combine.
6. Simmer until the peas are warm and the liquid is entirely absorbed (about 10 minutes).
7. Season with salt and pepper, to taste, and serve.

Nutrition information: per serving: 391 calories; 11.7 g fat; 22.3 g protein; 45.6 g carbohydrates; 12.5 g fiber

11. Paella with Artichokes and Peas

Paella with Artichokes and Peas is a delicious and flavorful traditional Spanish meal. It is full of fresh vegetables and savory flavors and spices, creating a unique and tantalizing dish.
Serving: 6
Preparation Time: 10 minutes
Ready time: 40 minutes

Ingredients:
- 2 tablespoons olive oil
- 3 cloves garlic, minced
- 1 diced onion
- 1 red bell pepper, diced
- 2 teaspoons smoked paprika
- 1/2 teaspoon turmeric
- 1 teaspoon cumin

- 1/2 teaspoon ground black pepper
- 1/4 teaspoon saffron threads
- 2 cups short grain rice
- 4 cups vegetable broth
- 1 can (14.5 oz) diced tomatoes
- 1 cup of artichoke hearts, drained
- 1/2 cup frozen peas
- Salt, to taste

Instructions:
1. Heat the olive oil in a large skillet over medium-high heat.
2. Add the garlic, onion, and bell pepper, stirring frequently until the vegetables are softened, about 5 minutes.
3. Add the spices - smoked paprika, turmeric, cumin, black pepper, and saffron - and cook for an additional 2 minutes.
4. Stir in the rice and cook, stirring regularly, for 1-2 minutes.
5. Pour in the broth and diced tomatoes and bring the mixture to a boil.
6. Reduce to a simmer and cook, stirring occasionally, until the rice is cooked, about 20 minutes.
7. Add the artichoke hearts and peas and continue cooking until the mixture is creamy and the vegetables are cooked through, about 5-10 minutes.
8. Taste and season with salt and additional spices as desired.
9. Serve and enjoy!

Nutrition information: Servings: 6; Calories: 306; Fat: 8g; Carbs: 46g; Protein: 8g

12. Paella with Green Beans and Asparagus

Paella with Green Beans and Asparagus is a flavorful one-pot meal that is perfect for a dinner party or for a weeknight dinner. It is quick and easy to make and can be served with any accompaniment.
Serving: 4
Preparation Time: 15 minutes
Ready Time: 45 minutes

Ingredients:

- 4 cups short-grain rice
- 2 tablespoons olive oil
- 1 onion, chopped
- 1 red bell pepper, diced
- 4 cloves garlic, minced
- 1 teaspoon smoked paprika
- 2 teaspoons ground cumin
- 8 cups vegetable broth
- 1 cup green beans, cut into 1" pieces
- 1 cup asparagus, cut into 1" pieces
- 1 teaspoon sea salt
- 1 teaspoon freshly ground black pepper

Instructions:
1. Heat the olive oil in a large pan or pot over medium heat.
2. Add the onion and bell pepper and cook, stirring occasionally, until softened, about 5 minutes.
3. Add the garlic, paprika, and cumin and stir to combine. Cook for 1 minute more.
4. Add the vegetable broth, green beans, asparagus, salt, and pepper. Stir to combine.
5. Increase the heat to high and bring the mixture to a boil.
6. Add the rice and stir to combine. Reduce the heat to low and simmer, uncovered, for 25 minutes, stirring occasionally.
7. Remove the pan from the heat and let it stand, uncovered, for 10 minutes before serving.

Nutrition information:
Calories: 396,Carbohydrates: 68g,Fat: 9g,Protein: 11g, Cholesterol: 0mg, Sodium: 1300mg.

13. Duck and Mushroom Paella

Duck and Mushroom Paella is a flavor-packed and hearty Spanish dish consisting of tender duck, flavorful mushrooms, and a mixture of aromatic spices cooked in a saffron flavoured risotto-style rice.
Serving: 4
Preparation Time: 10 minutes

Ready Time: 40 minutes

Ingredients:
- 2 duck breasts, skin-on and cubed
- 2 tablespoons olive oil
- 8 ounces cremini mushrooms, sliced
- 1 onion, chopped
- 2 cloves garlic, finely chopped
- 1 teaspoon smoked paprika
- Pinch of saffron
- 1 cup long-grain rice
- 2 cups hot chicken stock
- 1 bell pepper, chopped
- 2 tablespoons fresh parsley, chopped

Instructions:
1. Heat the oil in a large skillet or paella pan over medium-high heat.
2. Add the duck and cook for 5 minutes, stirring occasionally.
3. Add the mushrooms, onion, garlic, smoked paprika and saffron. Cook for 5 minutes more.
4. Add the rice and stir to combine.
5. Add the hot chicken stock and bell pepper.
6. Bring to a boil, cover the pan and reduce the heat to medium-low. Simmer for 20-25 minutes.
7. Uncover the pan and cook for 5 more minutes.
8. Sprinkle with fresh parsley and serve.

Nutrition information:
Calories per serving: 353 | Carbohydrates: 27g | Protein: 21g | Fat: 16g | Sodium: 667mg | Fiber: 2g

14. Paella with Roasted Red Peppers

Paella with Roasted Red Peppers is a flavorful Spanish dish that combines traditional Spanish flavors with a touch of sweetness from the roasted peppers. Served as a light meal or a side dish, this recipe is perfect for any occasion.
Serving: Serves 6

Preparation Time: 10 minutes
Ready Time: 40 minutes

Ingredients:
- 3 tablespoons olive oil
- 2 cloves garlic, minced
- 2 cups uncooked paella rice
- 4 cups vegetable broth
- 1 large onion, diced
- 2 cups sliced roasted red peppers
- 1 teaspoon smoked paprika
- 1 teaspoon ground cumin
- 1 teaspoon dried oregano
- Salt and pepper to taste
- 2 cups diced cooked chicken
- 1/2 cup frozen peas
- 2 tablespoons chopped fresh parsley

Instructions:
1. In a large sauté pan, heat the olive oil over medium heat.
2. Add the garlic and sauté for 1 minute. Add the rice and stir until all of the grains are coated with oil.
3. Add the vegetable broth and bring to a boil. Reduce the heat to low and stir in the onion, roasted red peppers, paprika, cumin, oregano, salt and pepper. Simmer, covered, for 20 minutes.
4. Add the chicken, peas, and parsley and stir for 1 to 2 minutes until heated through.
5. Serve hot.

Nutrition information: Each serving contains 280 calories, 9.2g fat, 29.2g carbohydrates, 3g fiber, 15.4g protein.

15. Paella with Clams and Mussels

Paella with Clams and Mussels is a delicious Spanish-style dish that combines some of the best seafood flavors. This dish is a flavorful combination of clams, mussels, and flavorful rice that will really make your taste buds sing!

Serving: 8
Preparation time: 45 minutes
Ready time: 1 hour

Ingredients:
- 2 tablespoons extra virgin olive oil
- 1 yellow onion, chopped
- 4 cloves garlic, minced
- 2 red bell peppers, chopped
- 2 cups arborio rice
- 4 cups low sodium chicken broth
- 1 can (14 ounces) diced tomatoes
- 1 teaspoon saffron threads
- Salt and freshly ground pepper
- 2 lbs clams, scrubbed
- 2 lbs mussels, debearded
- 1/4 cup fresh parsley, minced
- 1/4 cup sliced kalamata olives
- 2 tablespoons freshly squeezed lemon juice

Instructions:
1. Heat the olive oil over medium-high heat in a large sauté pan. Add the onion and garlic and cook for 2-3 minutes. Add the red bell peppers and cook for another 3-4 minutes.
2. Add the arborio rice and stir until the it is coated in the oil. Add the chicken broth, diced tomatoes, and saffron threads and bring to a boil. Lower the heat to medium-low and simmer for 15 minutes.
3. Add the clams and mussels to the pan and cook for another 6-7 minutes, until the clams and mussels open up. Season with salt and freshly ground pepper to taste.
4. Stir in the fresh parsley, kalamata olives, and lemon juice. Remove from heat and serve.

Nutrition information:
Calories: 350
Fat: 13 g
Carbohydrates: 44 g
Protein: 12 g
Sodium: 780 mg

16. Paella with Pork Ribs and Beans

Bursting with flavour, this Paella with Pork Ribs and Beans is the perfect comfort food! This classic Spanish dish is sure to become a family favourite and is easy to prepare.
Serving: 6-8
Preparation Time: 15 minutes
Ready Time: 45 minutes

Ingredients:
- 2 tablespoons olive oil
- 2 onions, chopped
- 4 garlic cloves, minced
- 2 teaspoons smoked paprika
- 1 teaspoon saffron threads
- 2 cups short grain rice
- 8-10 pork ribs
- 4 cups vegetable stock
- 2 cups cooked white beans
- 2 red peppers, diced
- 1 teaspoon sugar
- 2 lemons, cut into wedges
- Large pinch of sea salt

Instructions:
1. Preheat oven to 350°F (180°C).
2. Heat olive oil in a large, oven-safe skillet over medium-high heat. Add onions and cook until soft and translucent, about 5 minutes.
3. Add garlic and cook for a further 1 minute.
4. Add smoked paprika, saffron threads, rice and pork ribs. Cook for 2 minutes, stirring constantly.
5. Pour in vegetable stock and bring to a boil. Place the skillet in the preheated oven and cook uncovered for about 30 minutes, stirring occasionally.
6. Add white beans, red peppers, sugar and a pinch of sea salt. Return the skillet to the oven and cook for a further 15 minutes.
7. Serve the paella with wedges of lemon.

Nutrition information: Calories: 500; Protein: 25 g; Fat: 21 g; Carbohydrates: 48 g; Sodium: 800 mg; Sugar: 6 g; Fiber: 8 g

17. Paella with Rabbit and Snails

An authentic Spanish Paella with Rabbit and Snails - enjoy the traditional tastes of the Spanish countryside in this delicious dish!
Serving: 8
Preparation Time: 30 minutes
Ready Time: 90 minutes

Ingredients:
- 2lb Rabbit, cut in pieces
- 1lb Snails
- 5 cups Short-grain rice
- 2-3 bay leaves
- 2 Medium onions, chopped
- 4 cloves Garlic, minced
- 3 oz Tomatoes
- 1/4 cup Olive oil
- 2-3 cups Chicken broth
- 2 teaspoon Salt
- 1/2 teaspoon Pepper
- 2-3 teaspoons Fresh Parsley, minced

Instructions:
1. Heat oil in a large paella pan – or a large deep skillet - over medium heat.
2. Add Rabbit pieces and brown for 5-7 minutes.
3. Add Snails, Onions, and Garlic to the pan and cook for an additional 5 minutes.
4. Add Rice, Tomatoes, Chicken Broth, Salt, and Pepper to the pan and stir to combine everything.
5. Bring to a simmer and reduce heat to low. Cook, stirring often, until all of the liquid is absorbed, about 45 minutes.
6. Once the liquid has been absorbed, remove the pan from the heat and garnish with Parsley. Allow the Paella to rest for 15 minutes before serving.

Nutrition information:
Calories: 311 kcal; Total Fat: 11.2 g; Cholesterol: 41 mg; Sodium: 393 mg; Total Carbohydrates: 36.7 g; Protein: 12.9 g.

18. Paella with Octopus and Squid

Paella is a classic Spanish dish, made with rice, chicken, seafood, peppers, onions, and smoky Spanish paprika. This particular variation of Paella features octopus and squid, and is a traditional, yet flavorful treat.
Serving: 6
Preparation time: 15 minutes
Ready time: 40 minutes

Ingredients:
- 2 tablespoons olive oil
- 1/2 white onion, chopped
- 1 red bell pepper, chopped
- 1 teaspoon paprika
- Salt and pepper to taste
- 2 cloves garlic, minced
- 2 cups paella rice
- 8 cups chicken stock
- 1/2 lb squid, cleaned and cut into rings
- 1 octopus, cleaned and diced
- 1/2 cup peas

Instructions:
1. Heat olive oil in a large paella pan over medium-high heat.
2. Add the onion, bell pepper, paprika, salt and pepper, and garlic and cook until the vegetables are softened, about 4-5 minutes.
3. Add the rice and stir until it's coated in the oil.
4. Add the chicken stock and bring to a boil.
5. Reduce the heat to medium-low and simmer for 20 minutes.
6. Add the squid, octopus, and peas and simmer for an additional 5 minutes.
7. Turn off the heat and let the paella sit for 10 minutes before serving.

Nutrition information: per serving (6 servings total) – Calories: 340, Fat: 8g, Carbohydrates: 37g, Protein: 22g, Fiber: 2g

19. Paella with Chicken and Shrimp

Paella is a traditional Spanish dish made with saffron-infused rice, vegetables and often meats or seafood. This version of paella combines chicken and shrimp, making it a delicious, protein-filled meal.
Serving: 4
Preparation time: 15 minutes
Ready time: 40 minutes

Ingredients:
- 2 tablespoons olive oil
- 1 small onion, diced
- 3 cloves garlic, minced
- 1 teaspoon smoked paprika
- 1 teaspoon saffron threads
- 1 cup short-grained rice
- 2 cups chicken broth
- 2 large boneless, skinless chicken breasts, cut into 1-inch cubes
- 1/2 pound medium shrimp, peeled and deveined
- 1 red bell pepper, diced
- 1 cup frozen peas
- 1/2 cup chopped fresh parsley
- Salt and black pepper, to taste

Instructions:
1. Heat olive oil in a large skillet over medium heat.
2. Add onion and garlic; cook until softened, stirring occasionally, about 5 minutes.
3. Add smoked paprika and saffron, cook, stirring, for 1 minute.
4. Stir in rice and chicken broth. Bring to a simmer, reduce heat to low and cover.
5. Cook for 20 minutes.
6. Add chicken, shrimp, bell pepper, and peas; cook, stirring occasionally, until chicken and shrimp are cooked through, about 10 minutes.
7. Stir in parsley and season with salt and black pepper to taste.

8. Serve warm.

Nutrition information: Per serving: 273 calories; 8.7 g fat; 26.9 g carbohydrates; 20.7 g protein.

20. Paella with Lamb and Rosemary

This Spanish-style paella is a savory mix of tender lamb, aromatic herbs, and flavorful spices. It's sure to please any crowd and is a great dinner option to add to your weeknight repertoire!
Serving: 6
Preparation Time: 25 minutes
Ready Time: 1 hour

Ingredients:
- 1 tablespoon olive oil
- 1 large onion, diced
- 2 cloves garlic, minced
- 1 teaspoon smoked paprika
- 2 teaspoons dried oregano
- 1 ½ pounds boneless lamb shoulder, trimmed and cubed
- 2 cups short-grain rice
- 4 cups chicken broth
- 2 teaspoons of rosemary, chopped
- Salt and freshly ground black pepper, to taste
- 1 red bell pepper, seeded and diced
- 1 cup frozen peas, thawed

Instructions:
1. Heat the olive oil in a large pan over medium heat.
2. Add the onion, garlic, paprika, and oregano and season with salt and pepper. Cook, stirring occasionally, until the onion is softened.
3. Add the lamb and cook, stirring occasionally, until browned.
4. Add the rice, chicken broth, and rosemary and bring to a boil.
5. Reduce heat to low, cover, and simmer for 15 minutes.
6. Add the red pepper and snap peas and simmer, covered, for an additional 15 minutes or until the rice grains are tender and the liquid is absorbed.

Nutrition information:
Calories: 567 kcal, Carbohydrates: 54.0 g, Protein: 27.7 g, Fat: 20.8 g, Cholesterol: 87.0 mg, Sodium: 843.7 mg, Potassium: 369.8 mg, Fiber: 3.0 g, Sugar: 2.9 g

21. Paella with Spinach and Feta

Paella with Spinach and Feta is a delicious combination of flavors that will make your mouth water. The paella is made with aromatic spices, spinach, and salty feta cheese that all come together to create an unforgettable meal.
Serving: 4
Preparation time: 15 minutes
Ready time: 45 minutes

Ingredients:
2 teaspoons olive oil
1 onion, minced
4 cloves garlic, minced
2 cups paella rice
4 cups vegetable stock
1 teaspoon paprika
1/2 teaspoon sea salt
1/4 teaspoon black pepper
1/2 teaspoon saffron
3 cups fresh spinach
1 cup crumbled feta cheese

Instructions:
1. Heat olive oil in a large skillet over medium-high heat. Add onion and garlic and cook until lightly browned, about 5 minutes.
2. Add paella rice and stir to coat. Add vegetable stock, paprika, salt, pepper and saffron and bring to a boil.
3. Reduce heat to low and simmer until rice is tender, about 25 minutes.
4. Add spinach and stir until wilted.
5. Sprinkle with feta cheese and cover. Simmer for 10 minutes more.
6. Serve and enjoy.

Nutrition information: Per serving- 210 calories, 7 g fat, 27 g carbohydrates, 6 g protein, 210 mg sodium.

22. Paella with Chorizo and Prawns

Paella with Chorizo and Prawns is a colourful, tasty and comforting one-pot meal that is sure to impress family and friends.
Serving: 6
Preparation time: 10 minutes
Ready time: 45 minutes

Ingredients:
- 250g paella rice
- 3 garlic cloves, finely chopped
- 1 large onion, finely chopped
- 150g chorizo sausage, sliced
- 1 red bell pepper, diced
- 2 cloves
- 6 tomatoes, finely chopped
- 2 vegetable stock cubes
- 2 large pinches of saffron
- 1 litre boiling water
- 200g large raw prawns
- ½ lemon, juiced
- 2 tablespoons parsley, chopped

Instructions:
1. Heat some olive oil in a large deep frying pan or paella pan over a medium heat. Add the onion and garlic and cook until the onion is softened.
2. Add the chorizo and red pepper and cook until the chorizo begins to colour.
3. Add the rice, cloves, tomatoes, stock cubes, saffron and 1 litre of boiling water.
4. Bring to the boil and reduce to a low heat. Simmer for 25 minutes or until the liquid has been absorbed and the rice is cooked.

5. Add the prawns and lemon juice and cook for a further 5 minutes or until the prawns are cooked through.
6. Taste and adjust seasoning as necessary.
7. Sprinkle with chopped parsley and serve.

Nutrition information: per serving –
Calories: 544,
Carbs: 57g,
Fat: 16g,
Protein: 23g.

23. Paella with Calamari and Green Olives

Enjoy a Mediterranean flavor with this delicious paella dish with calamari and green olives.
Serving: 6
Preparation Time: 10 minutes
Ready Time: 45 minutes

Ingredients:
- 2 tbsp extra virgin olive oil
- 1 large onion, diced
- 2 cloves garlic, minced
- 2 cups long grain white rice
- 4 cups vegetable broth
- 1 large red bell pepper, diced
- 1 can (14.5oz) diced tomatoes
- 2 cups frozen green peas
- 1/4 tsp saffron threads
- 1/2 lb cleaned squid, diced
- 1/2 cup sliced green olives
- Salt and freshly ground black pepper to taste

Instructions:
1. Heat the olive oil over medium-high heat in a large skillet or paella pan.
2. Add the onion and garlic and sauté until the onion is translucent, about 5 minutes.

3. Add the rice and stir the mixture until the rice is lightly browned, about 5 minutes.
4. Add the vegetable broth, red bell pepper, tomatoes, green peas, and saffron. Bring the mixture to a boil and reduce the heat to low. Simmer for 20 minutes, stirring occasionally.
5. Add the calamari and green olives and simmer for an additional 10 minutes.
6. Season with salt and pepper and serve hot.

Nutrition information: Serving size: 1 cup; Calories: 300; Total Fat: 5g; Cholesterol: 20mg; Sodium: 610mg; Total Carbohydrates: 50g; Protein: 10g.

24. Paella with Salmon and Peppers

Paella with Salmon and Peppers is a traditional dish with a Spanish twist. This dish is a great way to mix vegetables, seafood and rice together for a complete and satisfying meal.
Serving: 4
Preparation Time: 15 minutes
Ready Time: 45 minutes

Ingredients:
- 2 tablespoons olive oil
- 1 onion, finely chopped
- 2 cloves garlic, minced
- 1 can diced tomatoes
- 1 1/2 cups short-grain Spanish rice
- 2 cups vegetable broth
- 1 teaspoon salt
- 1 teaspoon ground cumin
- 1/2 teaspoon paprika
- 1/2 teaspoon red pepper flakes
- 1 red bell pepper, seeded and chopped
- 1 yellow bell pepper, seeded and chopped
- 1 pound fresh salmon, cubed
- 1/4 cup fresh parsley, chopped

Instructions:
1. Heat the oil in a large skillet over medium-high heat.
Add the onion and garlic and cook, stirring occasionally, until the onion is translucent, about 5 minutes.
2. Add the tomatoes, rice, broth, salt, cumin, paprika, and red pepper. Bring the mixture to a boil, then reduce the heat to low and simmer, covered, for 25 minutes, stirring occasionally.
3. Add the bell peppers, salmon, and parsley and stir to combine. Simmer for an additional 10 minutes, stirring occasionally, until the bell peppers are tender and the salmon is cooked through.

Nutrition information:
Calories: 314
Total Fat: 8g
Saturated Fat: 1g
Cholesterol: 53mg
Sodium: 757mg
Total Carbohydrate: 33g
Dietary Fiber: 2g
Sugars: 4g
Protein: 22g

25. Paella with Beef and Peas

Paella with Beef and Peas is a traditional Spanish dish packed with flavor and classic Ingredients. This dish makes a delicious comfort food for any occasion.
Serving: 6
Preparation time: 30 minutes
Ready time: 1 hour 15 minutes

Ingredients:
- 2 tablespoons olive oil
- 1 large onion, diced
- 2 cloves garlic, minced
- 2 tablespoons smoked paprika
- 1 teaspoon ground cumin
- 1/2 teaspoon saffron threads

- 1/2 teaspoon dried oregano
- 1 pound skirt steak, sliced against the grain into thin strips
- Salt and freshly ground black pepper
- 1 teaspoon tomato paste
- 4 cups chicken broth
- 3/4 cup long-grain white rice
- 2 roasted red bell peppers, deseeded and diced
- 8 ounces frozen peas

Instructions:
1. Heat the olive oil in a large paella pan or cast-iron skillet over medium heat. Add the onion and garlic, and cook, stirring, until softened, about 5 minutes.
2. Add the paprika, cumin, saffron, and oregano and cook, stirring, for 1 minute.
3. Season the steak with salt and pepper and add to the pan. Cook, stirring, until lightly browned, about 3 minutes.
4. Add the tomato paste and cook, stirring, for 1 minute. Add the broth and bring to a boil.
5. Add the rice, bell peppers, and peas. Reduce the heat to low and cook, stirring occasionally, until the rice is cooked through, about 18 minutes.
6. Serve hot.

Nutrition information: 15g total fat, 6g saturated fat, 25g carbohydrates, 19g protein, 6g fiber

26. Paella with Zucchini and Eggplant

Paella with Zucchini and Eggplant is a flavorful one-pot dish that is packed with vegetables and flavor. This traditional Spanish dish is simple to make and can be served as a main or side dish.
Serving: 4
Preparation Time: 10 minutes
Ready Time: 40 minutes

Ingredients:
2 tablespoons olive oil
1 onion, chopped

2 cloves of garlic, minced
1 teaspoon sweet paprika
1/2 teaspoon hot smoked paprika
1/2 teaspoon ground cumin
1 cup Arborio or long-grain rice
2 cups vegetable broth
1 zucchini, diced
1 eggplant, diced
Salt and pepper, to taste

Instructions:
1. Heat the olive oil in a large pan or paella pan over medium heat. Add the onion and garlic and cook for 3-4 minutes until the onion is softened and lightly browned.
2. Add the paprika, cumin, and rice and stir to coat the rice in the spices.
3. Pour in the vegetable stock and bring to a boil. Add the diced zucchini and eggplant, reduce the heat, and simmer for 10 minutes until the vegetables are cooked through and the rice is tender.
4. Season with salt and pepper, taste, and adjust the seasoning if necessary.
5. Serve the Paella with Zucchini and Eggplant hot.

Nutrition information: Per Serving: Calorie: 183 kcal, Total Fat: 7 g, Saturated Fat: 1 g, Cholesterol: 0 mg, Sodium: 356 mg, Carbohydrates: 25 g, Fiber: 3 g, Sugar: 3 g, Protein: 4 g

27. Paella with Scallops and Bacon

A deliciously creamy and salty paella with succulent scallops, smoky bacon, tomatoes, and herbs.
Serving: 4 servings
Preparation Time: 20 minutes
Ready Time: 40 minutes

Ingredients:
- 2 tablespoons olive oil
- 6 ounces bacon, diced into small pieces
- 2 cloves garlic, minced

- 2 cups Arborio rice
- 6 cups chicken broth
- 1 cup dry white wine
- 1 teaspoon smoked paprika
- 1/2 teaspoon saffron threads
- 10 ounces scallops
- 1 cup chopped tomatoes
- 2 tablespoons chopped fresh parsley
- 1 teaspoon salt
- 1/2 teaspoon black pepper

Instructions:
1. Heat the olive oil in a large, deep skillet over medium-high heat. Add the bacon and cook, stirring occasionally, until the bacon is crisp and golden brown, about 8 minutes.
2. Add the garlic and cook for 1 minute. Add the rice and stir until lightly toasted, about 1 minute.
3. Add the chicken broth, wine, paprika, and saffron and bring to a boil. Reduce the heat to low and simmer, stirring occasionally, until most of the liquid has been absorbed, about 20 minutes.
4. Add the scallops, tomatoes, and parsley and continue to simmer until the scallops are cooked through and the liquid is completely absorbed, about 10 minutes.
5. Stir in the salt and pepper and remove from the heat. Serve hot.

Nutrition information: Calories 301, Total Fat 11 g, Saturated Fat 2 g, Cholesterol 20 mg, Sodium 1361 mg, Total Carbohydrate 34 g, Dietary Fiber 2 g, Sugars 1 g, Protein 11 g.

28. Paella with Cod and White Beans

Paella with Cod and White Beans is an amazing dish that combines succulent cod with healthy white beans in a delicious and flavorful rice dish. This delicious meal is sure to please both the health-conscious and the flavor-seekers.
Serving: 4
Preparation time: 10 minutes
Ready time: 45 minutes

Ingredients:
- 4 cod fillets
- 2 tablespoons olive oil
- 1 onion, chopped
- 2 cloves garlic, minced
- 2 cups white beans, cooked and drained
- 2 cups arborio rice
- 4 cups vegetable broth
- 1 teaspoon smoked paprika
- 2 tablespoons chopped parsley
- Salt and pepper to taste

Instructions:
1. Preheat oven to 350 degrees F.
2. Heat olive oil in a large oven-safe skillet over medium heat. Add onion and garlic, and cook until softened, about 3 minutes.
3. Add cooked and drained white beans, arborio rice, vegetable broth, smoked paprika, and parsley. Stir together until combined.
4. Place cod fillets on top of the rice and season with salt and pepper.
5. Simmer over medium-low heat for 20 minutes, stirring occasionally.
6. Transfer skillet to preheated oven and bake for 20 minutes until liquid is absorbed and cod is cooked through.
7. Serve with extra parsley and lemon wedges, if desired.

Nutrition information:
Calories: 346 calories, Carbohydrates: 45g, Protein: 18g, Fat: 10g, Saturated Fat: 2g, Cholesterol: 35mg, Sodium: 645mg, Potassium: 545mg, Fiber: 5g, Sugar: 3g, Vitamin A: 173IU, Vitamin C: 5mg, Calcium: 79mg, Iron: 3mg

29. Paella with Pork Tenderloin and Chorizo

A classic dish that is sure to be a crowd pleaser, Paella with Pork Tenderloin and Chorizo is the perfect dish for any special occasion. This dish is to die for with succulent pork, smoky chorizo, and flavorful vegetables cooked in a delicious saffron rice.
Serving: 4

Preparation time: 15 minutes
Ready time: 45 minutes

Ingredients:
- 1 teaspoon minced garlic
- ½ teaspoon smoked paprika
- 2 tablespoons olive oil
- 1 lb pork tenderloin, cut into 1 inch cubes
- 4 oz chorizo, sliced
- ½ onion, diced
- 1 bell pepper, diced
- 1 teaspoon saffron powder
- 3 cups chicken or vegetable stock
- 2 cups long-grain white rice
- 1 cup frozen peas

Instructions:
1. Preheat oven to 400°F.
2. In a large skillet, heat the olive oil over medium heat. Add the garlic, smoked paprika, and pork cubes and cook until the pork is lightly golden. Add the chorizo and cook until the pork is cooked through, about 7 minutes.
3. Add the onion, bell pepper, and saffron powder to the mixture and cook for another 5 minutes.
4. Add the stock and rice and mix well. Bring to a boil, reduce heat, cover, and simmer for 20 minutes.
5. Add the frozen peas and mix well. Transfer the mixture to a 9x13 baking dish. Bake in the preheated oven for 20-25 minutes, until the rice is tender and the mixture is bubbly.
6. Serve and enjoy!

Nutrition information: Calories – 383, Fat – 15 g, Carbohydrates – 35 g, Protein – 20 g, Sodium – 516 mg, Fiber – 2 g.

30. Paella with Green Peppers and Tomatoes

This delicious Paella with Green Peppers and Tomatoes features a Mediterranean-inspired flavor and a robust mix of colors. It's an excellent choice for a crowd-pleasing dinner or lunch.
Serving: 6
Preparation Time: 15 minutes
Ready Time: 45 minutes

Ingredients:
- 2 tablespoons olive oil
- 1 large onion, diced
- 2 red bell peppers, seeded and diced
- 2 cloves garlic, minced
- 1 teaspoon smoked paprika
- 2 teaspoons fresh oregano, chopped
- ½ teaspoon fine sea salt
- 2 cups Spanish or Arborio rice
- 2 3/4 cups vegetable broth
- 2 cups diced tomatoes
- 1 cup frozen green peas
- 1/2 cup green olives, pitted and chopped

Instructions:
1. Heat the oil in a large paella pan or extra deep skillet over medium-high heat and add the onion, bell peppers, garlic, paprika, oregano, and salt.
2. Cook the vegetables for 7-8 minutes, stirring occasionally until the pepper has softened and the onions are lightly golden.
3. Add the rice and cook another minute, stirring.
4. Add the vegetable broth and the tomatoes and stir. Bring to a boil, reduce to low heat, and simmer for 15 minutes.
5. Add the frozen green peas and olives and stir Ingredients together. Cover and cook for another 10 minutes, or until the rice is cooked and liquid is absorbed.

Nutrition information:
Calories per serving: 402; Total Fat: 9 g (1.5 g Saturated); Cholesterol: 0 mg; Sodium: 684 mg; Total Carbohydrate: 70 g; Dietary Fiber: 4 g; Protein: 8 g

31. Paella with Anchovies and Capers

Paella with Anchovies and Capers is a Spanish rice dish prepared with a blend of aromatics, spices, and bold flavors. This recipe is an update to the classic paella, with the addition of crunchy capers, salty anchovies, and white wine.

Serving: 8
Preparation Time: 15 minutes
Ready Time: 40 minutes

Ingredients:
- 2 tablespoons olive oil
- 8 cloves garlic
- 3 teaspoons Spanish paprika
- 4 cups chicken broth
- 1 teaspoon dried thyme
- 2 cups diced onion
- 1 can diced tomatoes
- 2 ½ cups short grain rice (preferred Arborio or Valencia rice)
- 8 ounces anchovies in oil
- ½ cup white wine (optional)
- 1 cup Capers (rinsed & drained)
- pinch of saffron
- 2 tablespoons chopped parsley

Instructions:
1. Heat 2 tablespoons of olive oil in a large skillet over medium-high heat.
2. Add the garlic and cook for 1 minute.
3. Add the Spanish paprika and stir to combine.
4. Add the chicken broth, thyme, onions, tomatoes, and rice and stir.
5. Bring the mixture to a boil, then reduce heat to low and simmer for 20 minutes or until all liquid is absorbed.
6. Add the anchovies, white wine, capers, and saffron and stir to combine.
7. Simmer for 10 minutes or until liquid is absorbed.
8. Serve hot and garnish with chopped parsley.

Nutrition information:
Calories: 305 kcal

Fat: 9 g
Carbohydrates: 38 g
Protein: 10 g
Sodium: 687 mg
Potassium: 263 mg
Fiber: 2 g
Sugar: 5 g

32. Paella with Shrimp and Chorizo

Paella with Shrimp and Chorizo is a classic Spanish dish, typically made with saffron rice, shrimp, chorizo, and peppers. It is a great dish for entertaining and can be easily customized according to preference.
Serving: 4
Preparation Time: 15 minutes
Ready Time: 40 minutes

Ingredients:
- 2 tablespoons olive oil
- 2 cloves garlic, minced
- 1 yellow onion, diced
- 2 chorizo sausages, diced
- 1 bell pepper, diced
- 1 teaspoon smoked paprika
- 1 teaspoon kosher salt
- 1/2 teaspoon freshly ground black pepper
- 1 cup long-grain rice
- 2 cups chicken broth
- 2 1/2 cups seafood stock
- 8 ounces medium shrimp, peeled and deveined
- 1/4 cup freshly chopped parsley
- 2 tablespoons freshly squeezed lemon juice

Instructions:
1. Heat the olive oil in a large pot over medium-high heat.
2. Add the garlic, onion, and chorizo and cook until the onion is soft and the chorizo is lightly browned.

3. Add the bell pepper, paprika, salt, and pepper and cook for an additional couple of minutes.
4. Add the rice and stir to combine.
5. Pour in the chicken broth and seafood stock and bring to a boil.
6. Reduce the heat to low, cover, and simmer for about 20 minutes.
7. Add the shrimp and cook until they are just cooked through, about 5 minutes.
8. Turn off the heat and stir in the parsley and lemon juice.

Nutrition information:
Calories: 360; Total Fat: 10g; Saturated Fat: 2g; Cholesterol: 109mg; Sodium: 1150mg; Carbohydrates: 41g; Fiber: 4g; Sugar: 3g; Protein: 20g.

33. Paella with Crab and Tomato

Paella is a classic Spanish dish that is made by combining rice, various types of seafood, and vegetables. This version of paella is made with crab, tomato, and other flavorful Ingredients, making it especially delicious. Enjoy this classic Spanish dish with friends and family!
Serving: 4
Preparation Time: 15 minutes
Ready Time: 30 minutes

Ingredients:
- 2 tablespoons olive oil
- 2 cloves garlic, minced
- 4 cups chicken stock
- 2 cups paella rice
- 1 medium tomato, diced
- 1½ cups cooked crab meat
- ¼ teaspoon paprika
- ¼ teaspoon cumin
- 1 teaspoon saffron
- 2 cups frozen peas, thawed

Instructions:
1. Heat the olive oil in a large paella pan over medium heat.
2. Add the garlic and cook for 1 minute.

3. Add the chicken stock, paella rice, tomato, and crab meat, and stir to combine.
4. Add the paprika, cumin, and saffron and stir to combine.
5. Bring the mixture to a boil.
6. Reduce the heat to low and simmer for 15 minutes, or until the rice has absorbed the liquid.
7. Add the peas and stir to combine.
8. Cook for an additional 10 minutes, or until the rice is tender.
9. Serve immediately.

Nutrition information:
Calories: 518 kcal, Carbohydrates: 58 g, Protein: 28 g, Fat: 19 g, Saturated Fat: 3 g, Cholesterol: 97 mg, Sodium: 1211 mg, Potassium: 637 mg, Fiber: 5 g, Sugar: 4 g, Vitamin A: 688 IU, Vitamin C: 23 mg, Calcium: 91 mg, Iron: 5 mg.

34. Paella with Chicken and Sausage

Paella with Chicken and Sausage is a delicious Mediterranean dish which combines Spanish saffron-flavored rice with chorizo and chicken. It is an easy and crowd-pleasing meal that pairs nicely with a glass of white wine.
Serving: 4
Preparation Time: 15 minutes
Ready Time: 45 minutes

Ingredients:
- 4-6 chicken thighs
- 2 cups Arborio rice
- 1 link of chorizo, diced
- 2 cloves garlic, minced
- 1 teaspoon Spanish paprika
- 1/2 teaspoon turmeric
- 1 teaspoon saffron
- 2 cups chicken stock
- 1 cup frozen peas
- 1/2 cup roasted red peppers, chopped
- 1/2 cup Parmesan cheese, shredded
- Salt and pepper to taste

Instructions:
1. Preheat the oven to 350 degrees F (175 degrees C).
2. Place the chicken thighs in an oven-safe baking dish and season with salt and pepper. Bake in the preheated oven until cooked through, about 25 minutes.
3. Meanwhile, heat a large skillet over medium-high heat. Add the chorizo and cook, stirring occasionally, until lightly browned, about 5 minutes.
4. Add the garlic, paprika, turmeric, and saffron and cook, stirring, for 1 minute.
5. Add the Arborio rice and stir to combine.
6. Pour the chicken stock into the skillet and bring to a boil.
7. Reduce the heat to low, cover, and simmer for 15 minutes or until the rice is cooked.
8. Uncover and stir in the peas, roasted red peppers, and Parmesan cheese.
9. Remove the chicken from the oven and add it to the skillet.
10. Serve with a glass of white wine.

Nutrition information: 156 calories; 7g fat; 14g carbohydrates; 8g protein; 1g fiber.

35. Paella with Baby Squid and Piquillo Peppers

This delicious and flavorful paella recipe with baby squid and piquillo peppers is a great option for a weekend dinner. It is packed with flavor and is the perfect meal for sharing with family and friends.
Serving: 6
Preparation Time: 20 minutes
Ready Time: 40-45 minutes

Ingredients:
- 1/4 cup extra-virgin olive oil
- 2 cloves garlic, chopped
- 2 cups Spanish-style rice
- 4 cups chicken stock
- 1 teaspoon smoked paprika

- 1 teaspoon saffron threads
- 1/2 pound baby squid, cleaned and cut into 1/2-inch pieces
- 1/2 pound piquillo peppers, roasted and peeled
- 1/2 cup frozen peas, thawed
- 1/4 cup fresh parsley, chopped

Instructions:
1. Heat a large paella pan or skillet over medium heat and add the oil. When hot, add the garlic and sauté for 1 minute.
2. Add the rice and stir until it is lightly toasted, about 5 minutes.
3. Pour in the chicken stock, paprika, and saffron and bring to a boil.
4. Reduce the heat to a simmer and add the squid, piquillo peppers, and peas.
5. Let the paella cook for about 25 minutes, until the rice is tender.
6. Remove the pan from the heat and sprinkle with the fresh parsley.
7. Serve the paella warm.

Nutrition information:
Calories: 350; Total Fat: 12g; Saturated Fat: 2g; Trans Fat: 0g; Mono Fat: 6g; Cholesterol: 40g; Sodium: 575mg; Potassium: 460mg; Total Carbohydrate: 41g; Dietary Fibre: 3g; Sugars: 3g; Protein: 15g

36. Paella with Sardines and Lemon

This pleasant aromatic Paella with Sardines and Lemon is packed with flavour and nutrition. It's a perfect dish to share with family or friends.
Serving: 6
Preparation time: 15 mins
Ready time: 45 mins

Ingredients:
- 500g paella or risotto rice
- 2 tablespoons olive oil
- 2 garlic cloves, crushed
- 4 lemons, zest finely grated and juice freshly squeezed
- 250g sardines, skinned and boned
- 500ml vegetable stock
- 4 tablespoons chopped flat-leaf parsley

• Salt and freshly ground black pepper, to taste

Instructions:
1. Heat the olive oil in a large non-stick pan over medium heat. Add the garlic and cook for 1-2 minutes, or until softened.
2. Add the rice and cook, stirring for 1-2 minutes, until the rice is glossy.
3. Add the lemon zest, lemon juice, sardines, and stock. Bring to the boil, then reduce the heat and simmer for 30 minutes, or until the rice is tender and the liquid has been absorbed.
4. Remove the pan from the heat and stir in the chopped parsley. Season to taste with salt and pepper.

Nutrition information: Per serving: Calories 186; Fat 4.33g; Saturated Fat 0.74g; Protein 7.4g; Carbohydrates 31.7g; Dietary Fiber 1.9g; Sugar 0.8g.

37. Paella with Veal and Artichokes

This delicious Spanish paella with veal and artichokes is cooked to perfection with flavorsome Ingredients.
Serving: 6
Preparation Time: 30 minutes
Ready Time: 55 minutes

Ingredients:
• 2 tablespoons olive oil
• 2 cloves garlic, minced
• 1/2 teaspoon paprika
• 1/4 teaspoon cumin
• 1 teaspoon dried oregano
• 2 cups chicken broth
• 3 cups arborio rice
• 2 cups diced veal
• 4 artichoke hearts, chopped
• 1 bell pepper, diced
• 1/2 cup frozen peas
• 1 tablespoon chopped fresh parsley

Instructions:
1. Heat oil in a large skillet over medium heat. Add garlic, paprika, cumin, and oregano; cook for 2 minutes.
2. Pour in broth and bring to a simmer. Add rice to the skillet and simmer for 10 minutes.
3. Add veal, artichoke hearts, bell pepper, and peas; simmer for 15 minutes.
4. Sprinkle with parsley and serve.

Nutrition information: Per serving: Calories 351, Total Fat 8g, Saturated Fat 2g, Cholesterol 75mg, Sodium 389mg, Carbohydrates 48g, Fiber 6g, Protein 21g.

38. Paella with Green Peas and Mint

This Paella with Green Peas and Mint is a classic Spanish dish that is simple yet full of flavor. The mint adds freshness to the dish and the green peas add color.
Serving: 6
Preparation time: 10 minutes
Ready Time: 25 minutes

Ingredients:
- Olive oil
- 2 cloves of garlic, minced
- 1 ½ cups of uncooked Arborio rice
- 1 teaspoon of ground turmeric
- 3 cups of vegetable broth
- 1 ½ cups of frozen green peas
- 2 tablespoons of fresh mint, chopped
- ½ cup of Parmesan cheese, grated
- Salt and pepper, to taste

Instructions:
1. Heat the olive oil in a large skillet over medium heat.
2. Add the garlic and cook for one minute.
3. Add the Arborio rice and turmeric and cook for one minute, stirring frequently.

4. Add the vegetable broth and stir.
5. Bring the mixture to a simmer and cook for 15 minutes, stirring occasionally.
6. Add the frozen green peas and stir.
7. Cook for an additional five minutes, stirring occasionally.
8. Remove from heat and stir in the fresh mint, Parmesan cheese, and salt and pepper.
9. Serve and enjoy!

Nutrition information:
Per serving: 242 Calories | 10g Fat | 29g Carbohydrates | 7g Protein

39. Paella with Duck and Figs

Paella with Duck and Figs is a traditional Spanish dish, packed with flavor and nutrition. Serve it with garlic toast for a complete meal.
Serving: 4
Preparation Time: 10 minutes
Ready Time: 45 minutes

Ingredients:
- 3 teaspoons olive oil
- 2 large onions, chopped
- 2 cloves garlic, minced
- 1 teaspoon dried oregano
- 2 cups long grain white rice
- 1/4 teaspoon smoked paprika
- 4 cups chicken broth
- 2 cups cooked, diced duck
- 12 dried figs, chopped
- 1 pinch saffron
- Salt, to taste
- Freshly ground black pepper, to taste

Instructions:
1. Heat the oil in a large paella pan over medium-high heat. Add the onion and cook until softened and lightly browned, about 5 minutes. Add the garlic and oregano and cook an additional minute.

2. Add the rice and paprika, stirring to coat the grains. Gradually add in the broth and bring the mixture to a boil. Reduce the heat to low and simmer, uncovered, until the rice is almost cooked through, about 15 minutes.
3. Add the duck, figs, and saffron. Simmer an additional 10 minutes, until the rice is fully cooked and most of the liquid has been absorbed.
4. Remove the paella from the heat, season with salt and pepper to taste, and let it rest for 5 minutes. Serve hot.

Nutrition information:
Calories: 388 kcal
Fat: 11 g
Carbohydrates: 56 g
Protein: 16 g
Sodium: 420 mg

40. Paella with Swordfish and Olives

Paella with Swordfish and Olives is a delicious Spanish seafood dish with a mix of flavors that come together in a flavorful and fragrant combination. As one of the most popular Mediterranean dishes, it's a great dish to enjoy with family and friends.
Serving: 4-6 people
Preparation time: 20 minutes
Ready time: 45 minutes

Ingredients:
- 2 tablespoons of olive oil
- 2 cloves of minced garlic
- 1 onion, chopped
- 3/4 cup of white rice
- 2 cups of chicken broth
- 2 cups of tomato sauce
- 12 ounces of swordfish, cut into cubes
- 1/2 cup of black olives, chopped
- Salt and pepper, to taste

Instructions:

1. Heat the olive oil in a large skillet over medium heat.
2. Add garlic and onion and sauté for about 5 minutes or until onion becomes tender.
3. Add the rice and mix with the garlic and onion until the rice begins to turn golden.
4. Pour in the chicken broth and tomato sauce and mix well.
5. Bring the mixture to a boil, reduce the heat to low and simmer for 15 minutes.
6. Add the swordfish, olives, salt and pepper, mix gently and cook for an additional 10 minutes.
7. Serve and enjoy!

Nutrition information: Per Serving (4-6 people): Calories 200, Fat 8 g, Saturated Fat 1 g, Cholesterol 26 mg, Sodium 201 mg, Carbohydrate 20 g, Fiber 2 g, Protein 18 g

41. Paella with Rabbit and Chickpeas

Paella with Rabbit and Chickpeas is a delicious Spanish dish, combining rabbit, chickpeas, and spices for an unforgettable flavor.
Serving: 4
Preparation time: 15 minutes
Ready time: 45 minutes

Ingredients:
- 2 tablespoons olive oil
- 2 cloves garlic, minced
- 2 cups diced rabbit
- 2 teaspoons paprika
- 1/2 teaspoon saffron threads
- 4 cups chicken stock
- 2 cups Bomba rice
- 1 cup cooked chickpeas
- 2 cups diced tomatoes
- 1 small red bell pepper, diced
- 2 tablespoons chopped fresh parsley

Instructions:

1. Heat the olive oil in a large pan over medium-high heat.
2. Add the garlic and rabbit and cook for 3-4 minutes, stirring often.
3. Add the paprika and saffron and cook for 1 minute, stirring constantly.
4. Add the chicken stock, rice, chickpeas, tomatoes, and bell pepper. Simmer for about 20-25 minutes, stirring occasionally.
5. Remove from heat and let stand for 5 minutes before serving.
6. Garnish with parsley.

Nutrition information: Per serving: 344 calories, 16g fat, 18g carbohydrate, 21g protein.

42. Paella with Shrimp and Green Beans

This classic Spanish seafood dish is an easy and flavorful dish with an impressive presentation, perfect for a memorable dinner any night.
Serving: 4
Preparation Time: 15 minutes
Ready Time: 40 minutes

Ingredients:
-2 tablespoons olive oil
-2 cloves garlic, minced
-½ onion, chopped
-1 teaspoon smoked paprika
-1 teaspoon cumin
-2 cups short-grain rice
-3 cups chicken stock
-1 bell pepper, chopped
-2 tomatoes, chopped
-2 cups green beans, cut into 1-inch pieces
-1 cup shrimp, peeled and deveined
-Salt and pepper, to taste

Instructions:
1. Heat oil in a large skillet over medium heat. Add garlic and onion and cook until softened, about 5 minutes.
2. Add paprika, cumin, rice, and chicken stock.

3. Bring the mixture to a boil then cover and reduce the heat. Simmer for 20 minutes.
4. Add bell pepper, tomatoes, and green beans. Cook uncovered for 10 minutes.
5. Add shrimp and season with salt and pepper to taste. Cook until shrimp are cooked through, about 5 minutes.

Nutrition information: Per serving (4): 397 calories, 16g fat, 31g protein, 27g carbs, 2g fiber, 7g sugars.

43. Paella with Lamb and Eggplant

Paella with Lamb and Eggplant is a delicious and nutritious Spanish dish, made with flavorful lamb, eggplant, and a variety of other Ingredients. This traditional dish is sure to impress your guests and family.
Serving: 8-10
Preparation Time: 20 minutes
Ready Time: 45 minutes

Ingredients:
- 2 ½ tablespoons olive oil
- 2 pounds ground lamb
- 2 large onions, diced
- 3 cloves garlic, minced
- 1 large green pepper, diced
- 2 large eggplants, cubed
- 1 teaspoon smoked paprika
- 2 teaspoons ground cumin
- 2 tablespoons tomato puree
- ½ cup frozen peas
- 2 cups Arborio rice
- 4 cups vegetable stock
- 2 tablespoons chopped parsley, for garnish

Instructions:
1. Heat the olive oil in a large skillet over medium heat.
2. Add the ground lamb and cook until the lamb is cooked through.
3. Add the onions and garlic and cook for 5 minutes, stirring frequently.

4. Add in the green pepper and eggplant and cook for another 5 minutes, stirring occasionally.
5. Add the smoked paprika, ground cumin, and tomato puree and stir to combine.
6. Add the frozen peas and Arborio rice, stirring to coat the rice.
7. Pour in the vegetable stock and bring to a simmer.
8. Reduce the heat and cover, simmering for 20 minutes until the rice is cooked.
9. Serve the paella with a sprinkle of chopped parsley.

Nutrition information: Per serving: Calories: 523 kcal, Carbohydrates: 68 g, Protein: 23 g, Fat: 19 g, Saturated Fat: 6.4 g, Sodium: 519 mg, Fiber: 9.3 g, Sugar: 4.9 g.

44. Paella with Clams and Chorizo

Paella with Clams and Chorizo is a classic Spanish dish that consists of a bed of rice cooked in a flavorful broth and topped with clams and chorizo. A unique mix of textures and bold flavors make this a memorable dish for any dinner.
Serving: Serves 6
Preparation time: 10 minutes
Ready time: 45 minutes

Ingredients:
- 4 cups short-grain rice
- 4 tablespoons olive oil
- 2 cloves garlic, chopped
- 1 onion, diced
- 2 bell peppers, diced
- 8 ounces Spanish chorizo, diced
- 2 teaspoons smoked paprika
- 2 cups chicken broth
- 2 cups clam juice
- 2 tablespoons tomato paste
- 2 dozen littleneck clams, scrubbed

Instructions:

1. Preheat the oven to 400°F.
2. In a large, oven-safe skillet, heat the olive oil over medium heat. Add the garlic, onion, bell peppers, and chorizo, and sauté until the vegetables are tender and the chorizo is beginning to brown.
3. Add the smoked paprika and stir to combine.
4. Add the rice and stir to coat with the oil and vegetables.
5. Pour in the chicken broth and clam juice and stir in the tomato paste.
6. Bring the mixture to a boil, reduce the heat to low, cover the skillet and simmer for 20 minutes.
7. Add the clams, stir gently, and bake in the oven for 15 minutes, or until the clams have opened and the rice is fully cooked.
8. Serve hot.

Nutrition information: Calories: 410, Fat: 15g, Saturated fat: 2.5g, Carbohydrates: 52g, Protein: 11g, Cholesterol: 15mg, Sodium: 570mg, Potassium: 360mg, Fiber: 2.5g, Sugar: 15g.

45. Paella with Pork and Pineapple

This vibrant and scrumptious Paella with Pork and Pineapple recipe will bring a delicious and unique flavor to your dinner table.
Serving: 8
Preparation time: 10 minutes
Ready time: 35 minutes

Ingredients:
-2 tablespoons olive oil
-7 ounces smoked pork, chopped
-1 onion, chopped
-6 ounces paella rice
-5 ounces Chorizo sausage
-2 cloves garlic, crushed
-14 ounces chicken broth
-14 ounces can of diced pineapple
-Ground black pepper, to taste

Instructions:
1. Heat the olive oil in a large and deep skillet over medium high heat.

2. Add the smoked pork and chopped onion and cook for 5 minutes or until the onion has softened.
3. Add the paella rice, chorizo sausage, crushed garlic and cook for another 5 minutes.
4. Pour in the chicken broth and diced pineapple and bring the mixture to a gentle simmer.
5. Cook, stirring every few minutes, for about 20 minutes or until all the broth is absorbed and the paella is cooked through.
6. Season the dish with the ground black pepper and serve immediately.

Nutrition information: Per serving (1/8): 354 calories, 18g fat, 17g protein, 32g carbohydrates, 1g dietary fiber.

46. Paella with Squid and Peas

Paella with Squid and Peas is a flavorful and beautiful dish to behold. The smoky flavor of the chorizo, the salty savoriness of the squid, and the sweetness of the peas all come together to create a memorable culinary experience.
Serving: Serves 8
Preparation time: 15 minutes
Ready time: 1 hour

Ingredients:
- 2 tablespoons extra-virgin olive oil
- 2 Spanish chorizo sausages, diced small
- 1 onion, chopped
- 2 garlic cloves, minced
- 2 1/2 cups short-grain Spanish rice
- 5 cups chicken broth
- 2 tablespoons smoked paprika
- 1 pinch saffron threads
- 1/2 cup peas
- 2 cups squid, cut into bite-size pieces
- Salt and pepper, to taste
- 2 tablespoons chopped fresh parsley

Instructions:

1. Heat olive oil in a large paella pan or deep skillet over medium-high heat. Add the chorizo and cook until slightly browned, about 5 minutes.
2. Add the onion and garlic and cook until softened, about 5 minutes.
3. Add the rice and stir to combine. Cook for 1 minute.
4. Add the chicken broth, paprika, saffron, and peas. Bring to a boil, then reduce to a simmer. Cook for 15 minutes.
5. Add the squid and cook until the rice is tender, about 10 minutes.
6. Season to taste with salt and pepper. Sprinkle with parsley and serve.

Nutrition information: Average nutritional information per serving: 390 Calories, 15 g Fat, 43 g Carbohydrates, and 12 g Protein.

47. Paella with Chicken and Peppers

Paella with Chicken and Peppers is a traditional Spanish recipe made with a variety of Ingredients such as chicken, peppers, vegetables, and rich, flavorful saffron rice. This makes for a delicious and hearty meal.
Serving: 6
Preparation time: 15 minutes
Ready time: 45 minutes

Ingredients:
- 2 tablespoons olive oil
- 1 onion, diced
- 2 cloves of garlic, minced
- 1 red bell pepper, diced
- 2 boneless, skinless chicken breasts, diced
- 1 teaspoon smoked paprika
- 1 teaspoon ground cumin
- 1/2 teaspoon dried oregano
- 1 cup long grain rice
- 2 cups chicken broth
- 1/2 teaspoon saffron threads
- 2 large tomatoes, diced
- 1/2 cup frozen peas
- 1/4 cup chopped parsley

Instructions:

1. Heat the olive oil in a large skillet or pan over medium-high heat.
2. Add the onion and bell pepper and saute until softened, about 5 minutes.
3. Add the garlic and chicken and cook for an additional 5 minutes.
4. Add the smoked paprika, cumin, and oregano and cook for 1 minute.
5. Add the rice and stir to combine.
6. Add the broth and saffron and stir to combine.
7. Reduce the heat to low, cover, and cook for 25 minutes or until the rice is cooked through.
8. Add the tomatoes, peas, and parsley and cook for an additional 5 minutes.

Nutrition information: 445 calories, 16g fat, 38g carbohydrates, 29g protein

48. Paella with Beef and Mushrooms

Paella with Beef and Mushrooms is a classic Spanish dish that is bursting with flavour! This recipe pairs beef and mushrooms with traditional paella Ingredients like saffron and Valencia rice, creating a unique and delicious meal.
Serving: 6
Preparation Time: 15 minutes
Ready Time: 45 minutes

Ingredients:
- 2 cups beef stock
- 1 tablespoon olive oil
- 1 brown onion, diced
- 2 cloves garlic, diced
- 2 cups paella rice
- 1 teaspoon sea salt
- Pinch of saffron
- ½ cup white wine
- 300g beef, cubed
- 200g sliced mushrooms
- 2 tablespoons chopped parsley

Instructions:
1. In a large saucepan, heat the beef stock over medium heat.
2. In a separate pan, heat the olive oil and add the onion and garlic, cooking until softened.
3. Add the paella rice, salt, and saffron, and cook whilst stirring for 2 minutes.
4. Pour in the white wine and continue to stir until completely absorbed.
5. Pour in the beef stock and bring to a simmer.
6. Add the beef and mushrooms, stirring gently to combine.
7. Cover and cook for 20 minutes or until the rice is cooked and all the liquid has been absorbed.
8. Garnish with chopped parsley and serve.

Nutrition information: Per serving: Calories: 472   Protein: 24g Total Fat: 11g   Carbohydrates: 52g   Fiber: 1.4g   Sugars: 2.4g Cholesterol: 43mg   Sodium: 786mg

49. Paella with Asparagus and Pesto

This is an easy and delicious Paella with Asparagus and Pesto.
Serving: 4
Preparation time: 20 minutes
Ready time: 45 minutes

Ingredients:
- 2 tablespoons olive oil
- 1 cup uncooked short grain rice
- 2 cloves garlic, minced
- 1 yellow onion, chopped
- 1 red bell pepper, chopped
- 1 teaspoon paprika
- 1 teaspoon saffron
- 2 cups chicken broth
- 1 cup frozen green peas
- 1 cup asparagus, cut into 1-inch pieces
- 1/4 cup prepared pesto
- Salt and pepper, to taste

Instructions:
1. Heat the oil in a large skillet over medium-high heat.
2. Add the rice, garlic, onion, bell pepper, paprika and saffron and cook until the rice is lightly toasted, about 2-3 minutes.
3. Stir in the chicken broth and bring to a boil. Reduce the heat to low and let simmer, covered, for about 20 minutes, until the rice is tender.
4. Add the peas, asparagus and pesto and season with salt and pepper, to taste. Simmer for an additional 10 minutes, or until the vegetables are cooked through.
5. Serve warm.

Nutrition information: Per serving: 360 calories, 23g fat (2.5g saturated fat), 11g fiber, 17g protein, 29g carbohydrates, 8mg cholesterol, 363mg sodium.

50. Paella with Lobster and Tomatoes

Paella with Lobster and Tomatoes is a Spanish dish that is full of flavor and nutrition, making it the perfect meal to enjoy throughout the year.
Serving: 8
Preparation time: 30 minutes
Ready time: 1 hour 30 minutes

Ingredients:
- 800g uncooked bomba or short-grain rice
- 1.5l fish or chicken stock
- 4 medium ripe tomatoes, diced
- 8 lobster tails , cooked
- 2 tablespoons tomato paste
- 2 cloves garlic, minced
- 1 red onion, chopped
- 2 tablespoons olive oil
- 2 teaspoons paprika
- 2 teaspoons fresh oregano leaves
- 1 bay leaf
- Salt & pepper to taste

Instructions:

1. Heat olive oil in a large skillet over medium heat.
2. Add garlic and onion to the pan and sauté until fragrant, about 5 minutes.
3. Add the tomatoes, tomato paste, paprika, oregano, bay leaf, salt and pepper. Sauté for an additional 5 minutes.
4. Add the rice and stir until it is completely coated in the tomato mixture. Cook for an additional 5 minutes.
5. Pour in the stock and bring to a boil.
6. Reduce heat to low and simmer for 25 minutes, stirring occasionally, until the rice is cooked through and most of the liquid has been absorbed.
7. Add the lobster tails and cook for an additional 5 minutes.
8. Serve immediately.

Nutrition information: Per Serving: Calories: 398, Protein: 26g, Fat: 13g, Carbs: 36g, Sodium: 637mg

51. Paella with Sausage and Peppers

This delectable paella recipe is filled with savory sausage, crunchy peppers, and saffron-infused rice. A true Spanish classic, this colorful dish is sure to be a hit with everyone.
Serving: Makes 6 servings
Preparation Time: 15 minutes
Ready Time: 1 hour

Ingredients:
- 1 tablespoon olive oil
- 1 large onion, diced
- 1 red bell pepper, diced
- 8 ounces smoked sausage, sliced
- 1 teaspoon smoked paprika
- 1 teaspoon garlic powder
- 2 cups short-grain rice
- 2 cups vegetable broth
- 2 cups water
- ½ teaspoon saffron threads
- ½ teaspoon salt

- ¼ teaspoon freshly ground black pepper
- 2 bay leaves
- 2 lemons, thinly sliced

Instructions:
1. Heat the olive oil in a large pan over medium heat.
2. Add the onion and bell pepper and cook until softened, about 5 minutes.
3. Add the sausage and cook until lightly browned, about 5 minutes more.
4. Add the smoked paprika and garlic powder and stir to combine.
5. Add the rice and stir to combine.
6. Add the vegetable broth, water, saffron threads, salt, black pepper, and bay leaves. Stir to combine and bring to a boil.
7. Reduce the heat to low, cover, and simmer for 20 minutes.
8. Uncover and add the lemon slices. Cover and cook for an additional 10 minutes.
9. Remove from the heat and let sit for 10 minutes.
10. Fluff the paella with a fork and serve.

Nutrition information:
Calories: 380; Total Fat: 9g; Saturated Fat: 2g; Cholesterol: 21mg; Sodium: 860mg; Carbohydrates: 56g; Fiber: 4g; Protein: 10g.

52. Paella with Cod and Chickpeas

Paella with Cod and Chickpeas is a traditional Spanish dish created with simple Ingredients like rice, saffron, vegetables, and seafood. Enjoy its memorable flavours, texture, and colours and serve it with a nice glass of wine as a meal for long lunches and dinners for family and friends.
Serving: Serves 4
Preparation Time: 25 minutes
Ready Time: 1 hour 5 minutes

Ingredients:
- 4 tablespoons extra-virgin olive oil
- 1 onion, chopped
- 1 red pepper, chopped

- 2 cloves garlic, chopped
- 1 teaspoon paprika
- 1 teaspoon saffron
- 2 cups long-grain rice
- 4 cups chicken or vegetable broth
- 2 cups cooked chickpeas
- 2 cooked cod fillets, flaked
- 2 teaspoons chopped parsley
- Salt and pepper to taste

Instructions:
1. Heat the oil in a large, deep skillet over medium heat.
2. Add the chopped onion and red pepper and cook until softened, about 8 minutes.
3. Add the garlic, paprika, and saffron and cook for another minute.
4. Stir in the rice and cook, stirring, for 1 minute.
5. Add the broth and season with salt and pepper.
6. Bring the mixture to a boil, reduce the heat to low, and simmer for 15 minutes.
7. Add the chickpeas and cook for 10 minutes more, or until the rice is tender and the liquid is absorbed.
8. Add the fish flakes and parsley and cook for 1 minute more.
9. Serve the paella hot.

Nutrition information:
Calories: 311kcal, Carbohydrates: 45g, Protein: 17g, Fat: 7g, Saturated Fat: 1g, Cholesterol: 39mg, Sodium: 773mg, Potassium: 467mg, Fiber: 6g, Sugar: 3g, Vitamin A: 1159IU, Vitamin C: 56mg, Calcium: 67mg, Iron: 2mg

53. Paella with Pork and Cauliflower

Try this flavorful and easy-to-prepare Paella with Pork and Cauliflower dish, bursting with classic Mediterranean flavors!
Serving: 4
Preparation Time: 15 minutes
Ready Time: 35 minutes

Ingredients:
- 2 tablespoons olive oil
- 2 tablespoons paprika, divided
- 1 pound boneless pork loin, cut into 1-inch cubes
- 1 large onion, finely chopped
- 1 red bell pepper, finely chopped
- 2 garlic cloves, finely chopped
- 8 ounces white button mushrooms, quartered
- 2 cups cauliflower florets
- 2 cups long grain white rice
- 4 cups chicken stock
- 2 tablespoons chopped fresh parsley
- 1 teaspoon salt

Instructions:
1. Heat the olive oil in a large skillet over medium-high heat. Sprinkle the pork with 1 tablespoon of the paprika and cook for 5-7 minutes, stirring occasionally, until the pork is lightly browned.
2. Add the onion, red bell pepper, garlic, mushrooms, and cauliflower and cook for 5 minutes until the vegetables are tender.
3. Add the rice and stir to combine. Add the chicken stock, remaining tablespoon of paprika, parsley, and salt. Bring to a boil, then reduce the heat to low, cover and simmer for 20 minutes until the rice is tender and the liquid is absorbed.
4. Remove from the heat and let rest for 5 minutes before serving.

Nutrition information: Per Serving: Calories: 426, Protein: 27g, Total Fat: 8g, Cholesterol: 65mg, Sodium: 1152mg, Total Carbohydrate: 49g, Dietary Fiber: 2g

54. Paella with Shrimp and Asparagus

Paella with Shrimp and Asparagus is a classic Spanish dish that combines the best of savory and flavorful Ingredients into a delicious meal. This traditional dish is perfect for a party or a special gathering and is sure to please a crowd.
Serving: Serves 4
Preparation Time: 15 minutes

Ready Time: 40 minutes

Ingredients:
- 2 tablespoons of olive oil
- 1 onion, diced
- 1 red bell pepper, diced
- 2 cloves of garlic, minced
- 1 teaspoon of smoked paprika
- 2 cups of Arborio rice
- 24 ounces of chicken broth
- 12 ounces of frozen peas
- 1/2 teaspoon of saffron threads
- 2 bay leaves
- 1 pound of raw shrimp, peeled and deveined
- 1 cup of asparagus, cut into 1-inch pieces
- 2 tablespoons of chopped parsley
- 1 lemon, cut into wedges

Instructions:
1. Heat the olive oil in a large skillet over medium heat.
2. Add the onion and bell pepper, and cook until softened, about 3 minutes.
3. Add the garlic, paprika, and rice, and stir to combine.
4. Add the chicken broth, peas, saffron, and bay leaves, and bring to a boil.
5. Reduce heat to simmer and cover with a lid. Cook for 20 minutes, or until the broth is absorbed.
6. Uncover the skillet and add the shrimp and asparagus. Cook until the shrimp are cooked through and the asparagus is tender, about 10 minutes.
7. Stir in the chopped parsley and season with salt and pepper.
8. Serve with lemon wedges.

Nutrition information: Per serving: 402 calories; 16 g fat; 40 g carbohydrates; 26 g protein; 804 mg sodium; 4 g fiber.

55. Paella with Chicken and Green Olives

This Paella with Chicken and Green Olives recipe is a classic Spanish dish with saffron and tender rice--a great crowd-pleaser!
Serving: 4
Preparation Time: 15 minutes
Ready Time: 1 hour

Ingredients:
- 2 tablespoons olive oil
- 1 onion, diced
- 3 cloves garlic, minced
- 1 red bell pepper, diced
- 2 teaspoons smoked paprika
- 1 teaspoon ground cumin
- 1/2 teaspoon crushed red pepper flakes
- 2 cups long grain white rice
- 4 cups chicken broth
- 4 chicken thighs, cut into small pieces
- Salt and pepper, to taste
- 1/2 cup green olives, pitted
- 2 tablespoons chopped fresh parsley

Instructions:
1. Heat the oil in a large saucepan over medium-high heat. Add the onion and red pepper and cook until softened, about 5 minutes.
2. Add the garlic, paprika, cumin, pepper flakes, and rice and cook, stirring, until the rice is lightly toasted, about 3 minutes.
3. Add the chicken broth and bring the mixture to a boil.
4. Add the chicken and season with salt and pepper. Reduce the heat to low and simmer until the chicken is cooked through and the liquid is absorbed, about 40 minutes.
5. Add the green olives and stir to combine.
6. Serve the paella with fresh parsley, if desired.

Nutrition information:
Calories: 442,Fat: 17g,Saturated Fat: 4g,Carbohydrates: 38g,Fiber: 2g,Protein: 28g,Sodium: 784mg,Cholesterol: 81mg

56. Paella with Lamb and Mint

Paella is a classic Spanish dish traditionally made with rice, saffron, and a variety of meats and vegetables. This version of paella features lamb and mint for an added hint of herbiness.
Serving: 4
Preparation time: 10 minutes
Ready time: 1 hour

Ingredients:
- 2 tablespoons of olive oil
- 1 medium onion, diced
- 2 cloves of garlic, minced
- 2 teaspoons of smoked paprika
- 1/2 teaspoon of hot smoked paprika
- 1/2 teaspoon of sea salt
- 2 cups of short-grain rice
- 4 cups of chicken stock
- 2 pounds of boneless lamb, diced
- 1 teaspoon of fresh mint, chopped
- 2 tomatoes, diced

Instructions:
1. Heat the olive oil in a large skillet over medium-high heat.
2. Add the onions and garlic and cook until softened, about 5 minutes.
3. Add the paprikas, salt, and rice and cook, stirring, for 1 minute.
4. Pour in the chicken stock and bring to a boil.
5. Reduce the heat to low and simmer, covered, for 15 minutes.
6. Add the lamb and tomatoes and cook, covered, for 10 minutes more.
7. Remove the paella from the heat and stir in the mint.
8. Cover and let sit for 5 minutes before serving.

Nutrition information:
- Calories: 530 kcal
- Fat: 28 g
- Carbohydrates: 37 g
- Protein: 33 g
- Sodium: 1290 mg

57. Paella with Spinach and Chickpeas

This flavor-packed vegetarian version of classic paella is made with spinach, chickpeas and the perfect blend of spices. It is sure to please even the pickiest eaters and make a great centerpiece to any meal.
Serving: 6
Preparation Time: 10 minutes
Ready Time: 45 minutes

Ingredients:
- 2 tablespoons olive oil
- 2 cloves garlic, minced
- 1 onion, chopped
- 2 ½ cups vegetable broth
- 1 teaspoon saffron threads
- 2 tablespoons tomato paste
- ½ teaspoon paprika
- ½ teaspoon smoked paprika
- 1 cup short grain rice
- 2 cups cooked chickpeas
- 2 cups baby spinach, chopped
- 1 cup frozen peas
- 1 lemon, juiced
- Salt and pepper, to taste

Instructions:
1. In a large sauté pan, heat the olive oil over medium heat. Add the garlic and onion and cook until softened, about 5 minutes.
2. Add the vegetable broth, saffron, tomato paste, paprika and smoked paprika and stir to combine. Bring the mixture to a simmer.
3. Add the rice and stir to combine. Cover the pan and cook for 20 minutes, stirring occasionally.
4. Uncover the pan and add the chickpeas, spinach, peas, lemon juice and salt and pepper to taste. Cook for an additional 10 minutes, stirring occasionally.
5. Serve the paella hot.

Nutrition information:
Calories: 275 Protein: 8 g Carbohydrates: 46 g Dietary Fiber: 8 g Fat: 6 g Saturated Fat: 1 g Cholesterol: 0 mg Sodium: 766 mg

58. Paella with Clams and Spinach

This Paella with Clams and Spinach has a flavorful combination of fresh spinach with sweet clams makes this paella a flavorful addition to any dinner table.
Serving: Serves 4
Preparation time: 10 minutes
Ready time: 45 minutes

Ingredients:
- 1/2 cup olive oil
- 1 medium onion, finely diced
- 1 teaspoon minced garlic
- 1 pound fresh clams, cleaned
- 1 cup Arborio rice
- 1/4 cup white wine
- 2 cups low-sodium chicken or vegetable broth
- 1/2 teaspoon smoked paprika
- 1/4 teaspoon ground black pepper
- 1 cup fresh baby spinach, chopped
- 2 tablespoons parsley, chopped

Instructions:
1. Heat the olive oil in a large sauté pan over medium heat.
2. Add the onion and garlic, cooking for 2-3 minutes.
3. Add the clams and cook for another 2-3 minutes.
4. Add the rice and stir to combine.
5. Add the white wine and broth, stirring to combine.
6. Add the smoked paprika, black pepper, and spinach, stirring to combine.
7. Cover and reduce the heat to low. Cook for 20-25 minutes, or until the liquid is absorbed.
8. Remove from heat and let rest for 5 minutes.
9. Garnish with chopped parsley and serve.

Nutrition information: Calories: 371; Total fat: 10.5g; Sodium: 243mg; Carbohydrates: 18.1g; Protein: 8.7g; Cholesterol: 35mg.

59. Paella with Duck and Orange

Paella with Duck and Orange is a unique and delicious Spanish dish. The classic Ingredients are combined with orange and duck to deliver an amazing flavor. Serving: 6 Preparation Time: 30 minutes Ready Time: 1 hour

Ingredients:
- 1½ kg duck (cut into cubes)
- 2 tsp paprika
- 2 oranges (quartered)
- 400 g paella rice
- 80 ml olive oil
- 2 large tomatoes (peeled and diced)
- 2 onions (chopped)
- 1 garlic clove (minced)
- 500 ml chicken stock
- ½ tsp saffron threads
- Salt and pepper

Instructions:
1. Heat the olive oil in a large pan and add the duck cubes. Fry for 4-5 minutes until browned all over.
2. Add the onions, garlic and paprika and fry for a further 2-3 minutes.
3. Add the tomatoes, orange quarters, rice and chicken stock and stir until everything is well mixed.
4. Cover the pan with a lid and leave to cook over a low heat for 30 minutes, checking occasionally.
5. Add the saffron threads, season with salt and pepper and let the paella cook for an additional 15 minutes.
6. Serve the paella with duck and orange and enjoy.

Nutrition information:
Calories: 600 kcal, Protein: 25 g, Fat: 25 g, Carbohydrates: 54 g, Fiber: 6 g, Sugar: 9 g, Sodium: 600 mg

60. Paella with Swordfish and Peppers

Paella with Swordfish and Peppers is a tasty traditional Spanish dish that combines juicy swordfish with a variety of peppers and colorful vegetable accompaniments. It is a hearty and flavorful meal that is sure to satisfy.

Serving: 4-6
Preparation Time: 15 minutes
Ready Time: 35 minutes

Ingredients:
- 4 tablespoons olive oil
- 1 onion, finely chopped
- 2 cloves garlic, chopped
- 2 green bell peppers, diced
- 2 red bell peppers, diced
- 2 cups paella rice
- 4 cups chicken broth
- 1 teaspoon saffron threads
- 1 teaspoon sweet paprika
- 1 teaspoon smoked paprika
- 2 bay leaves
- 1 teaspoon sea salt
- 1/2 teaspoon freshly ground black pepper
- 500g swordfish, cut into cubes
- 1 large tomato, diced
- 2 tablespoons fresh parsley, chopped
- 2 tablespoons fresh oregano, chopped

Instructions:
1. Heat the olive oil in a large paella pan or a large heavy-bottomed skillet on medium-high heat. Add the onions and garlic and sauté for 3 minutes.
2. Add the bell peppers and continue sautéing for another 2 minutes.
3. Stir in the paella rice and cook for about 1 minute.
4. Add the chicken broth, saffron, sweet and smoked paprika's, bay leaves, salt, and pepper. Bring the mixture to a boil.
5. Reduce the heat and simmer for 15 minutes.
6. Add the swordfish cubes and tomato and simmer for another 5 minutes.

7. Sprinkle with parsley and oregano and cover the pan. Cook for a final 5 minutes or until the rice is fully cooked.

Nutrition information: Per serving: 469 calories, 20g fat, 5.6g saturated fat, 54g carbohydrates, 3g dietary fiber, 15g protein.

61. Paella with Rabbit and Green Beans

Paella with Rabbit and Green Beans is a traditional Valencian dish. It is a flavorful and satisfying combination of tender rabbit and crisp green beans, cooked in fragrant rice.
Serving: 4 servings
Preparation Time: 15 minutes
Ready Time: 35 minutes

Ingredients:
- 2 tablespoons olive oil
- 4 skinless rabbit legs, cut into small pieces
- 1 onion, diced
- 2 cloves garlic, minced
- 1 teaspoon smoked paprika
- 1 teaspoon ground cumin
- 1 teaspoon ground turmeric
- Salt and freshly ground black pepper to taste
- 2 cups short grain rice
- 4 cups chicken broth
- 1 cup green beans, cut into 1-inch pieces

Instructions:
1. Heat the oil in a large skillet over medium-high heat.
2. Add the rabbit pieces and cook for 8-10 minutes, or until lightly browned.
3. Add the onion and garlic, and cook for 5 minutes or until the onion is translucent.
4. Add the paprika, cumin, turmeric, salt and pepper and stir to combine.
5. Add the rice and stir for 1 minute.
6. Add the broth and bring to a boil.
7. Reduce the heat to low, cover the skillet and simmer for 20 minutes.

8. Add the green beans to the skillet, stir to combine and cook for an additional 10 minutes or until the liquid is absorbed.
9. Serve hot.

Nutrition information:
Calories: 442 calories,
Carbohydrates: 58.3 g,
Protein: 18.3 g,
Fat: 15.2 g,
Saturated Fat: 2.8 g,
Cholesterol: 43 mg,
Sodium: 46 mg,
Potassium: 787 mg,
Fiber: 3.6 g,
Sugar: 5.6 g

62. Paella with Crab and Corn

Paella with Crab and Corn is a classic Spanish dish that combines a variety of tastes and Ingredients in a delicious, comforting entree. The combination of sweet, juicy crab and sweet corn is harmonious and delightful.
Serving: 4
Preparation Time: 25 minutes
Ready Time: 35 minutes

Ingredients:
- 2 tablespoons olive oil
- 1 onion, diced
- 2 cloves garlic, minced
- 2 cups paella rice
- 4 cups vegetable broth
- 1 teaspoon paprika
- 1/2 teaspoon turmeric
- 1/4 teaspoon cayenne pepper
- 1 red bell pepper, diced
- 2 cups frozen corn
- 1 cup cooked crab meat

- 2 tablespoons fresh parsley, chopped

Instructions:
1. Heat the olive oil in a large skillet or paella pan over medium-high heat.
2. Add the onion and garlic and cook until softened, about 5 minutes.
3. Add the paella rice and stir to combine.
4. Add the broth, paprika, turmeric, and cayenne pepper. Bring to a boil.
5. Reduce heat to medium-low and simmer until the rice is just cooked, about 15 minutes.
6. Add the bell pepper and corn and cook until the vegetables are tender, about 5 minutes.
7. Stir in the crab meat and parsley and cook until heated through.
8. Serve and enjoy!

Nutrition information:
Per Serving: 313 calories; 3.4 g fat; 44.9 g carbohydrates; 17.1 g protein; 4.2 g fiber.

63. Paella with Chicken and Leeks

Paella with Chicken and Leeks is a classic Spanish dish that is incredibly easy and delicious. It is a flavorful mix of chicken, leeks, and rice cooked in a stew of tomatoes, garlic, and saffron. Perfect for a comforting dinner!
Serving: 4
Preparation Time: 15 minutes
Ready Time: 45 minutes

Ingredients:
- 2 tablespoons olive oil
- 1 leek, thinly sliced
- 2 cloves garlic, minced
- 2 boneless, skinless chicken breasts, cubed
- 2 cups uncooked long-grain white rice
- 2 cups chicken broth
- 1 teaspoon paprika
- 2 teaspoons saffron threads

- 2 tomatoes, diced
- 1/4 cup frozen peas
- 1/4 cup dry white wine, optional

Instructions:
1. Heat the olive oil in a large, deep skillet over medium heat. Add the leek and garlic and cook, stirring occasionally, for 3-4 minutes until softened.
2. Add the chicken and cook for 3-4 minutes until lightly browned.
3. Add the rice and stir to coat with the oil. Add the chicken broth, paprika, and saffron. Bring to a simmer, then reduce the heat to low, cover, and cook for 25 minutes.
4. Add the tomatoes, peas, and white wine. Stir to combine and re-cover the skillet. Cook for an additional 15 minutes, or until the rice is tender and the liquid has been absorbed.

Nutrition information:
Per Serving: Calories: 321, Total Fat: 6g, Saturated Fat: 2g, Cholesterol: 60mg, Sodium: 340mg, Carbohydrates: 43g, Fiber: 4g, Sugar: 3g, Protein: 22g

64. Paella with Veal and Mushrooms

Paella with Veal and Mushrooms is a unique Spanish dish bursting with fresh Ingredients such as vegetables, meats, and spices. This flavorful dish is great for making for large groups and comes together quickly.
Serving: Serves 6
Preparation Time: 10 minutes
Ready Time: 50 minutes

Ingredients:
- 2 tablespoons olive oil
- 1 red onion, diced
- 2 cloves garlic, minced
- 2 cups veal, cubed
- 1 cup mushrooms, sliced
- 1 green bell pepper, diced
- 2 cups long-grain white rice

- 4 cups chicken or vegetable broth
- 1 teaspoon paprika
- 1 teaspoon oregano
- 1 teaspoon smoked paprika
- 2 tablespoons parsley, chopped
- Salt to Taste

Instructions:
1. In a large skillet over medium-high heat, add olive oil.
2. Add red onion and garlic, stirring until fragrant, about 1 minute.
3. Add veal pieces and mushrooms and cook for 3 minutes, stirring often.
4. Add bell pepper and cook for another 3 minutes.
5. Add rice and cook for 2 minutes.
6. Add broth and all spices, stirring to combine.
7. Bring to a boil, reduce heat and simmer for 40 minutes, stirring occasionally.
8. When rice is cooked, turn off heat and stir in parsley.

Nutrition information: Calories: 340, Total Fat: 8.7g, Cholesterol: 40mg, Sodium: 730mg, Total Carbohydrates: 41g, Fiber: 1.9g, Sugar: 2g, Protein: 20.4g

65. Paella with Green Peas and Sausage

Paella with Green Peas and Sausage is a classic Spanish dish made with a flavorful saffron-infused rice, green peas, and sausage. It's easy to make and perfect for a weeknight dinner.

Serving: 6
Preparation time: 10 minutes
Ready time: 35 minutes

Ingredients:
- 2 Tbsp olive oil
- 2 cloves garlic, minced
- 1 lb chorizo, cut into ½ inch pieces
- 1 cup green peas
- 2 cups Spanish rice

- 3 cups vegetable broth
- 2 tsp paprika
- 1 tsp saffron
- Salt and pepper, to taste
- ½ cup parsley, chopped

Instructions:
1. Heat the olive oil in a large skillet over medium heat. Add the garlic and cook for 1 minute.
2. Add the chorizo and cook until lightly browned, about 5 minutes.
3. Add the green peas and cook for 1 minute.
4. Add the rice and stir to combine.
5. Add the broth, paprika, and saffron and season with salt and pepper.
6. Bring to a boil, reduce heat to low, cover and simmer for 20 minutes.
7. Garnish with parsley and serve.

Nutrition information:
- Calories: 351
- Fat: 19.9g
- Carbs: 31.4g
- Protein: 13.7g

66. Paella with Shrimp and Zucchini

Try this delicious paella with shrimp and zucchini! It's packed with flavors and guaranteed to impress your family and guests.
Serving: 6-8
Preparation time: 25 mins
Ready time: 1 hour

Ingredients:
- 2 tablespoons of olive oil
- 2 cloves of garlic, minced
- 1 yellow onion, chopped
- 1 cup of long grain white rice
- 2 cups of chicken broth
- 1 teaspoon of ground saffron
- 1 teaspoon of crushed red pepper flakes

- 12 ounces of peeled and deveined shrimp
- 1 cup of cubed zucchini
- 1 cup of roasted red peppers, diced
- 1 teaspoon of salt
- 1 teaspoon of freshly ground black pepper

Instructions:
1. Heat olive oil in a large skillet over medium-high heat.
Add garlic and onion. Cook for about 5 minutes.
2. Add rice and chicken broth. Stir to combine and bring to a boil.
3. Add saffron, red pepper flakes, shrimp, zucchini, roasted red peppers, salt, and pepper.
Stir and reduce heat to low.
4. Cover the skillet and simmer until the shrimp are cooked through and the rice is tender, about 20-25 minutes.

Nutrition information:
Calories: 224 kcal
Total Fat: 6.7 g
Saturated Fat: 1 g
Cholesterol: 72 mg
Sodium: 827 mg
Total Carbohydrate: 25.8 g
Dietary Fiber: 1.7 g
Sugars: 3.6 g
Protein: 14.4 g

67. Paella with Lamb and Caramelized Onions

Paella with Lamb and Caramelized Onions is a Mediterranean family meal with a savory combination of flavors. This quick and easy dish comes together quickly in one pot and is sure to leave everyone happy and full!
Serving: Serves 6
Preparation Time: 10 minutes
Ready Time: 35 minutes

Ingredients:

- 2 tablespoons extra-virgin olive oil
- 2 sweet onions, halved and thinly sliced
- 2 cloves minced garlic
- 2 teaspoons smoked paprika
- 2 cups basmati rice
- 2 cups chicken broth
- 2 cups lamb stock
- 1 teaspoon saffron threads
- 2 ½ cups diced tomatoes, drained
- 2 cups cooked lamb, cut into cubes
- 1 cup frozen peas
- 2 tablespoons chopped fresh parsley
- Salt and pepper to taste

Instructions:
1. Heat the oil in a large skillet over medium heat.
2. Add onions and sauté until softened and golden brown, about 8 minutes. Add garlic and smoked paprika and cook for an additional minute.
3. Add rice to the skillet and cook for a few minutes until lightly toasted.
4. Add chicken broth, lamb stock and saffron threads, and bring to a boil. Reduce heat to low, cover and let simmer for 15 minutes.
5. Uncover and stir in diced tomatoes, cooked lamb, and frozen peas. Continue to cook, stirring occasionally, for another 5-7 minutes, or until the rice is cooked through and the liquid has been absorbed.
6. Remove from heat and stir in parsley. Add salt and pepper to taste.

Nutrition information: Calories: 466, Fat: 13 g, Saturated Fat: 4 g, Cholesterol: 107 mg, Sodium: 596 mg, Carbohydrates: 51 g, Fiber: 4 g, Sugar: 7 g, Protein: 29 g

68. Paella with Clams and Piquillo Peppers

Paella with Clams and Piquillo Peppers is a seafood-focused variation of the classic Spanish rice dish that is both delicious and nutritious. Bursting with bright flavor, this recipe incorporates plump clams and sweet piquillo peppers to create a truly unique and memorable meal.
Serving: 4

Preparation Time: 15 minutes
Ready Time: 40 minutes

Ingredients:
-2 tablespoons olive oil
-1 onion, finely chopped
-2 cloves garlic, minced
-2 cups short-grain Spanish rice
-Kosher salt
-3 cups low-sodium chicken broth
-2 teaspoons smoked paprika
-1/2 teaspoon turmeric
-2 tablespoons tomato paste
-1 pound clams, scrubbed
-1 14-ounce jar of piquillo peppers, drained and thinly sliced
-1/4 cup chopped parsley
-Lemon wedges

Instructions:
1. Heat the oil in a paella pan or large skillet over medium heat. Add the onion and garlic and cook until softened, about 5 minutes.
2. Add the rice and 1 teaspoon of salt and cook, stirring occasionally, until lightly toasted, about 3 minutes.
3. Stir in the broth, paprika, turmeric, and tomato paste. Bring to a simmer and cook for 12 minutes.
4. Add the clams and piquillo peppers to the pan, cover and cook until the clams open, about 10 minutes.
5. Sprinkle with parsley, season with additional salt to taste, and serve with lemon wedges.

Nutrition information:
Calories: 393, Total Fat: 9 g, Saturated Fat: 2 g, Trans Fat: 0 g, Cholesterol: 37 mg, Sodium: 1447 mg, Carbohydrates: 61 g, Fiber: 3 g, Sugar: 5 g, Protein: 16 g

69. Paella with Pork and Apples

Paella with Pork and Apples is a flavorful dish that combines the tastes of savory pork and tart apples. It's cooked with saffron, giving it a slightly sweet flavor that pairs well with the rich pork.

Serving: 4
Preparation time: 10 minutes
Ready time: 50 minutes

Ingredients:
- 2 tablespoons olive oil
- 1 medium onion, diced
- 2 cloves garlic, minced
- 2 cups uncooked rice
- 4 cups chicken broth
- 1 teaspoon saffron threads
- 1/2 teaspoon salt
- 1/4 teaspoon black pepper
- 1 pound pork tenderloin, cut into 1-inch cubes
- 1 large apple, cored and diced
- 1/4 cup slivered almonds
- 2 tablespoons chopped parsley

Instructions:
1. In a large saucepan over medium heat, heat oil. Add onion and garlic and cook until softened, about 5 minutes.
2. Add rice and stir until lightly toasted, about 2 minutes.
3. Add chicken broth, saffron, salt, and pepper and bring to a boil.
4. Reduce heat to a simmer and stir in pork, apple, and almonds. Simmer for 30 minutes, stirring occasionally.
5. Remove from heat and stir in parsley. Cover and let stand for 10 minutes before serving.

Nutrition information: Per Serving: 332 calories, 10g fat, 29g protein, 32g carbohydrates, 4g fiber, 491mg sodium

70. Paella with Squid and Tomatoes

Paella with Squid and Tomatoes is a traditional Spanish dish, combining fragrant Arborio rice, seafood and vegetables. It's full of flavor and sure to delight your taste buds.

Serving: 4
Preparation Time: 10 minutes
Ready Time: 40 minutes

Ingredients:
- 2 tablespoons olive oil
- 1 medium onion, finely chopped
- 1 red pepper, cut into small chunks
- 2 cloves garlic, finely chopped
- 2 tablespoons sweet smoked paprika
- 2 cups long grain rice
- 4 cups chicken broth
- 2 large tomatoes, diced
- 1 lb squid, cleaned and cut into rings
- Salt and pepper to taste

Instructions:
1. Heat the oil in a large pot over medium heat.
2. Add the onion and pepper and cook for 3 minutes until softened.
3. Add the garlic and paprika and cook for an additional minute.
4. Add the rice and stir to coat with the oil and vegetables.
5. Add the chicken broth and bring to a boil, then reduce to a simmer.
6. Add the tomatoes and squid. Simmer for 25 minutes, stirring occasionally, until the rice is tender.
7. Season with salt and pepper to taste.

Nutrition information:
Calories: 330 | Fat: 4g | Sodium: 590mg | Carbohydrate: 43g | Fiber: 3g | Protein: 20g

71. Paella with Chicken and Mushrooms

Paella with Chicken and Mushrooms is a flavorful dish made with saffron-flavored rice, chicken, and mushrooms. This Spanish dish makes for a great meal when entertaining friends or family.

Serving: Serves 6
Preparation time: 20 minutes
Ready time: 45 minutes

Ingredients:
- 2 tablespoons olive oil
- 3 cloves garlic, minced
- 1 onion, diced
- 1 red bell pepper, diced
- 2 cups Arborio rice
- 8 cups chicken broth
- 2 teaspoons paprika
- 1 teaspoon dried oregano
- 2 cups chopped cooked chicken
- 2 cups sliced mushrooms
- 1 teaspoon saffron threads
- 1/2 teaspoon salt
- 2 tablespoons chopped fresh parsley

Instructions:
1. In a large pan, heat oil over medium heat. Add garlic, onion and bell pepper and cook for 3-4 minutes, stirring occasionally, until vegetables are softened.
2. Add rice and stir to coat with oil. Cook for 1 minute.
3. Add chicken broth, paprika, oregano, chicken, mushrooms, saffron and salt. Bring to a boil, reduce heat and simmer, covered, until rice is tender, about 20 minutes.
4. Stir in parsley and serve.

Nutrition information: Calories: 296, Total Fat: 6g, Cholesterol: 34mg, Sodium: 856mg, Total Carbohydrates: 41g, Dietary Fiber: 2g, Protein: 15g

72. Paella with Beef and Green Beans

This paella with beef and green beans is a flavorful and aromatic one-pot dish with a variety of textures. The Ingredients used in this dish come together to create an exciting and wholesome meal.

Serving: Makes 6 servings
Preparation time: 15 minutes
Ready time: 45 minutes

Ingredients:
- 2 tablespoons olive oil
- 2 cloves garlic, minced
- 1 large onion, chopped
- 1 pound beef, cut into cubes
- 2 cups beef broth
- 2 cups long-grain rice
- 1 teaspoon saffron
- 4 cups green beans, halved
- 2 tablespoons parsley, minced
- Salt and pepper to taste

Instructions:
1. Heat olive oil in a large pot over medium-high heat.
2. Add the garlic and onion and cook until softened.
3. Add the beef cubes and cook until browned, about 5 minutes.
4. Add the beef broth, rice, saffron, green beans, and parsley.
5. Season with salt and pepper to taste.
6. Bring to a boil, then reduce heat to low and cover.
7. Simmer for 20 minutes, until the liquid is absorbed and the rice is cooked through.
8. Serve, and enjoy!

Nutrition information:
Per serving: calories 331, fat 13g, saturated fat 4g, fiber 4g, protein 21g, carbohydrates 32g.

73. Paella with Asparagus and Sun-Dried Tomatoes

Paella with Asparagus and Sun-Dried Tomatoes is a classic Spanish dish bursting with flavor. The addition of asparagus and sun-dried tomatoes provides an extra depth of flavor and nutrition.
Serving: 4
Preparation Time: 15 mins

Ready Time: 45 mins

Ingredients:
- 2 cups short grain rice
- 2 tablespoons olive oil
- 1 cup diced onions
- 1 red bell pepper, diced
- 4 cloves of garlic, minced
- 2 teaspoons smoked paprika
- 1 teaspoon saffron threads
- 4 cups vegetable broth
- 1 lb asparagus, cut into 1 inch pieces
- ½ cup sun-dried tomatoes, chopped
- 1 teaspoon sea salt
- 1 lemon, juiced
- 2 tablespoons chopped fresh parsley

Instructions:
1. Heat the olive oil in a large paella pan over medium heat. Add the onions and bell pepper and sauté for 3-4 minutes or until softened.
2. Add the garlic, smoked paprika, and saffron and sauté for another 2 minutes.
3. Add the rice and stir to combine.
4. Add the broth and bring to a boil. Reduce heat to low and simmer for 20 minutes or until the rice is nearly cooked through.
5. Add the asparagus, sun-dried tomatoes, sea salt, and lemon juice and stir to combine. Cover and simmer for 10-15 minutes or until the rice is cooked through.
6. Remove from the heat and garnish with fresh parsley. Serve immediately.

Nutrition information: Per serving (1/4 of total): 355 calories, 11 g fat, 59 g carbohydrates, 7 g protein

74. Paella with Lobster and Corn

A classic Spanish dish, Paella with Lobster and Corn is a delicious one-pot meal that is flavoured with paprika, saffron and tomato.

Serving: Serves 4
Preparation Time: 10 minutes
Ready Time: 45 minutes

Ingredients:
- 2 tablespoons of olive oil
- 1 onion, finely chopped
- 2 garlic cloves, minced
- 2 cups of bomba rice
- 1/2 teaspoon of smoked paprika
- Pinch of saffron
- 4 cups of vegetable or chicken broth
- 1 (14.5-ounce) can fire-roasted diced tomatoes
- 2 cups of fresh or frozen corn
- 1 small cooked lobster, cut into bite-sized pieces
- 1/2 cup of peas
- 1/4 cup of fresh parsley, chopped
- Salt, to taste

Instructions:
1. Heat the oil in a large skillet over medium-high heat. Add the onion and garlic and cook until softened, approximately 3-4 minutes.
2. Add the rice, paprika and saffron. Cook, stirring, for 1 minute.
3. Add in the broth and tomatoes and bring to a boil. Once boiling, reduce the heat to low and cover. Simmer for 20 minutes.
4. Add the corn, lobster, peas, parsley and salt. Simmer for an additional 10 minutes or until the rice is tender and the liquid is absorbed.
5. Serve hot and enjoy.

Nutrition information: Per serving: 394 calories; 9.7g fat; 7.1g saturated fat; 217mg sodium; 53.2g carbohydrate; 4.8g fiber; 7.2g sugar; 25.0g protein.

75. Paella with Sausage and Eggplant

Paella with Sausage and Eggplant is a very delightful recipe with a deliciously warm taste. It is highly flavorful and a sure favorite for anyone who loves rice dishes.

Serving: 6
Preparation Time: 20 minutes
Ready Time: 45 minutes

Ingredients:
- 1 tablespoon olive oil
- 1 small onion, chopped
- 2 cloves garlic, minced
- 1 cup diced tomatoes
- 1/2 teaspoon pepper
- 1 teaspoon smoked paprika
- 2 cups diced eggplant
- 12 ounces cooked sausage, cut into pieces
- 2 cups uncooked white rice
- 2 1/2 cups chicken broth
- 1 1/2 cups peas
- Salt to taste

Instructions:
1. Heat the olive oil in a large pot over medium-high heat.
2. Add the onion and garlic and cook for 2 minutes, stirring often.
3. Add the diced tomatoes, pepper, smoked paprika, eggplant, sausage, and rice.
4. Stir to combine.
5. Pour in the chicken broth and bring to a low boil.
6. Reduce the heat to low and cover. Simmer for 20 minutes, or until the liquid has been absorbed and the rice is cooked through.
7. Add the peas and season with salt to taste.
8. Serve hot.

Nutrition information: 275 calories, 7g fat, 33g carbohydrate, 11g protein, 4g fiber

76. Paella with Cod and Potatoes

This delicious one-pan dish, Paella with Cod and Potatoes, is an easy and hearty meal that combines the flavors of Spanish cuisine.
Serving: Serves 4

Preparation Time: 10 minutes
Ready Time: About 25 minutes

Ingredients:
- ½ onion, diced
- 1 garlic clove, minced
- 1 teaspoon smoked paprika
- 2 tablespoons olive oil
- 6 ounces of cod fillets, cut into 1 inch cubes
- ¾ cup long-grain white rice
- 2 medium potatoes, cubed
- 1 ½ cups chicken broth
- 2 tablespoons fresh parsley, chopped
- Salt and pepper to taste

Instructions:
1. Begin by heating a large skillet over medium heat.
2. Add the onion, garlic, and smoked paprika, and sauté for about 2 minutes.
3. Add the olive oil, cod, and rice, and continue to cook for another 3 minutes until the cod is almost cooked.
4. Add the potatoes, and stir to combine everything.
5. Pour in the chicken broth, and bring the mixture to a boil.
6. Reduce the heat to low, and simmer for about 15 minutes, or until the liquid has been absorbed and the rice and potatoes are both cooked.
7. Turn off the heat, and stir in the parsley.
8. Season with salt and pepper, and serve.

Nutrition information:
Serving size: ⅛ of the recipe
Calories: 209
Total Fat: 7.8g
Saturated Fat: 1.2g
Cholesterol: 31mg
Sodium: 495mg
Carbohydrates: 24.5g
Fiber: 2.0g
Sugar:1.5g
Protein: 10.5g

77. Paella with Pork and Red Peppers

Paella with Pork and Red Peppers is a traditional Spanish dish, a favorite at paella parties all around the world. It combines the smoky flavor of the pork with the sweet and smoky flavor of the red peppers to create a delicious meal.

Serving: 4
Preparation Time: 15 minutes
Ready Time: 45 minutes

Ingredients:
- 2 tablespoons olive oil
- 1 onion, diced
- 4 cloves garlic, minced
- 2 cups uncooked paella rice
- 1 teaspoon smoked paprika
- 1/2 teaspoon saffron
- 4 cups chicken stock
- 12 ounces pork, diced
- 2 red peppers, diced
- 1 cup frozen peas
- 2 tablespoons chopped fresh parsley

Instructions:
1. Heat olive oil in a large skillet over medium heat. Add onion and cook for 3 minutes, or until tender. Add garlic and cook for 1 minute.
2. Add the paella rice, smoked paprika, and saffron; stir to combine.
3. Add the chicken stock and bring to a boil. Reduce heat to low, cover, and simmer for 15 minutes.
4. Add the diced pork, red peppers, and frozen peas. Cover and simmer for 15-20 minutes, or until the rice is cooked through.
5. Remove from heat and stir in the parsley.

Nutrition information: Per serving approx. 230 calories, 8g fat, 8g protein, 30g carbohydrate (s), 300mg sodium

78. Paella with Shrimp and Spinach

This flavorful Spanish dish of paella is prepared with shrimp and spinach for a delicious main course.
Serving: 4
Preparation time: 20 minutes
Ready time: 40 minutes

Ingredients:
1 ½ cups of short-grain paella rice
¼ cup of olive oil
3 cups of shrimp stock or clam juice
½ teaspoon of Aleppo pepper
1 teaspoon of smoked Spanish paprika
¼ teaspoon of saffron threads
1 large onion, finely chopped
4 cloves of garlic, minced
2 plum tomatoes, finely chopped
2 tablespoons of tomato paste
1 pound of peeled and deveined shrimp
2 cups of tightly packed spinach leaves
Salt and freshly ground black pepper to taste

Instructions:
1. Preheat oven to 350°F and lightly grease a large ovenproof skillet or paella pan.
2. Heat the olive oil over medium heat in the skillet or pan.
3. Add the onion and garlic and cook until onions are softened and fragrant, about 5 minutes.
4. Stir in the paprika, pepper, and saffron threads and cook for 1 minute.
5. Add the rice and stir for 1 minute.
6. Add the shrimp stock or clam juice and tomato paste and bring to a simmer.
7. Simmer for 5 minutes.
8. Spread the shrimp, tomatoes, and spinach over the top of the paella.
9. Transfer the skillet or pan to the preheated oven and bake for 20 minutes.
10. Turn off the heat and let the paella sit for 10 minutes.
11. Season with salt and pepper to taste before serving.

Nutrition information: 452 calories; 20g fat; 44g carbohydrates; 19g protein; 2g fiber.

79. Paella with Chicken and Piquillo Peppers

Paella with Chicken and Piquillo Peppers is a delicious and easy-to-make rice dish made with chicken, chorizo, piquillo peppers, and saffron. It is a flavorful and nutritious dish that is sure to please even the pickiest of eaters.

Serving: 4-6
Preparation Time: 15 minutes
Ready Time: 45 minutes

Ingredients:
- 4 tablespoons olive oil
- 2 boneless and skinless chicken breasts, cut into cubes
- 1/2 cup diced Spanish chorizo
- 1 small onion, finely chopped
- 2 cloves garlic, minced
- 1 cup short-grain rice (such as Arborio or Valencia)
- 2 cups chicken stock
- 1/2 teaspoon saffron threads
- 2 piquillo peppers, diced
- salt and freshly ground black pepper, to taste

Instructions:
1. Heat the olive oil in a large skillet over medium heat. Add the chicken and chorizo and season with salt and pepper. Cook until chicken is just cooked through, about 8 minutes.
2. Add the onion and garlic and cook for another 2 minutes.
3. Add the rice and stir to combine.
4. Pour in the chicken stock and add the saffron. Bring to a boil, then reduce the heat to low. Cover and cook for 20 minutes.
5. Add the piquillo peppers and stir to combine. Cover and cook for another 5 minutes.
6. Remove the skillet from the heat and let rest for 10 minutes. Fluff the paella with a fork before serving.

Nutrition information: Per Serving: 240 calories, 10g fat, 22g carbohydrates, 14g protein

80. Paella with Lamb and Garlic

Paella with Lamb and Garlic is a classic Spanish dish that is full of irresistible flavors. This traditional recipe will surely become a family favorite.
Serving: 4
Preparation time: 15 minutes
Ready time: 1 hour

Ingredients:
- 1/4 cup extra-virgin olive oil
- 3 cloves garlic, minced
- 1 medium onion, chopped
- 1 tablespoon smoked paprika
- 1 teaspoon saffron
- 2 cups Arborio rice
- 1/2 pound lamb stew, diced
- 1 cup peas
- 4 cups chicken stock
- 2 tomatoes, chopped
- 1/4 teaspoon salt
- 1/4 teaspoon black pepper

Instructions:
1. Heat the olive oil in a large skillet over medium heat.
2. Add the garlic, onion, paprika, and saffron. Cook, stirring, until soft, about 5 minutes.
3. Add the rice and stir for 2 minutes.
4. Add the lamb, peas, chicken stock, tomatoes, salt, and pepper.
5. Increase the heat and bring the mixture to a boil.
6. Reduce the heat to low and cover. Simmer for 30 to 40 minutes, or until the rice is tender and most of the liquid is absorbed.
7. Serve hot.

Nutrition information:

Calories: 487kcal, Carbohydrates: 62g, Protein: 18g, Fat: 18g, Sodium: 1202mg, Potassium: 523mg, Fiber: 6g, Sugar: 8g, Vitamin A: 955IU, Vitamin C: 37.4mg, Calcium: 88mg, Iron: 4.9mg.

81. Paella with Green Peas and Bacon

Paella with Green Peas and Bacon is a classic Spanish dish consisting of a flavorful rice medley that is filled with delicate vegetables and salty chunks of bacon. It is sure to be a crowd favorite!
Serving: 4-6
Preparation time: 10 minutes
Ready time: 1 hour

Ingredients:
- 2 tablespoons olive oil
- 2 cloves garlic, minced
- 1 medium onion, diced
- 2 cups long-grain white rice
- 4 cups vegetable or chicken broth
- 1 teaspoon smoked paprika
- 1 bay leaf
- Salt and freshly ground black pepper, to taste
- 1/2 cup frozen green peas
- 2 strips bacon, cooked and crumbled

Instructions:
1. Heat the oil in a large skillet over medium-high heat. Add the garlic and onion and cook for 5 minutes, stirring occasionally.
2. Add the rice and stir to combine. Cook for 1 minute.
3. Add the broth and bring to a boil. Add the paprika, bay leaf, salt, and pepper. Reduce the heat to low and simmer, stirring occasionally, for 30 minutes.
4. Add the peas and bacon and simmer for 10 minutes more, or until the rice is tender.

Nutrition information: Calories: 347; Protein: 9g; Total fat: 10.6g; Cholesterol: 13mg; Sodium: 578.4mg; Total carbohydrates: 49.6g; Fiber: 2.5g; Sugars: 2.6g

82. Paella with Clams and Bell Peppers

Paella with Clams and Bell Peppers is a classic Spanish dish that incorporates savory and succulent seafood along with bell peppers and other aromatics for a flavor-packed meal.

Serving: 4
Preparation Time: 15 minutes
Ready Time: 30 minutes

Ingredients:
- 2 tablespoons olive oil
- 1 medium onion, finely chopped
- 1 red bell pepper, stemmed, seeded, and chopped
- 2 cloves garlic, minced
- 1 teaspoon smoked paprika
- 8 ounces chorizo sausage, diced
- 2 cups Arborio rice
- 4 cups seafood stock
- 2 tablespoons tomato paste
- 1 cup frozen peas, thawed
- 1 pound clams, scrubbed
- Chopped fresh parsley, for garnish

Instructions:
1. Heat the olive oil in a large skillet over medium heat. Add the onion, bell pepper and garlic. Cook, stirring occasionally, until the vegetables are softened, about 5 minutes.
2. Add the smoked paprika and chorizo. Cook for 3 minutes more.
3. Add the Arborio rice and stir to coat. Cook for 1 minute.
4. Add the seafood stock, tomato paste, and frozen peas. Bring to a simmer and cook for 10 minutes.
5. Add the clams and cook, stirring occasionally, until the clams have opened and the rice is tender, 10 to 12 minutes more.
6. Serve garnished with parsley.

Nutrition information:

Per Serving: 390 Calories; 16g Fat; 27g Carbohydrates; 28g Protein; 6g Fiber; 797mg Sodium

83. Paella with Duck and Mushrooms

Paella with Duck and Mushrooms is a traditional Spanish rice dish that is full of flavor and really simple to make. This version features flavorful duck and earthy mushrooms for a unique and delicious take on this classic dish.
Serving: 4
Preparation Time: 10 minutes
Ready Time: 40 minutes

Ingredients:
- 2 tablespoons olive oil
- 8 ounces duck, cut into 1/2 inch pieces
- 1 medium onion, finely chopped
- 1/2 teaspoon Spanish smoked paprika
- 2 cloves garlic, finely chopped
- 8 ounces mushrooms, chopped
- 1/2 teaspoon salt
- 2 cups uncooked paella rice
- 4 cups chicken stock
- 1/4 teaspoon saffron threads
- 1/4 cup frozen peas

Instructions:
1. Heat the olive oil in a large skillet over medium heat. Add the duck and cook, stirring occasionally, until golden brown and crispy, about 8 minutes.
2. Add the onions, paprika, garlic, mushrooms, and salt to the skillet. Cook, stirring occasionally, until the vegetables are soft, about 5 minutes.
3. Add the paella rice, stirring to coat with the oil from the skillet. Pour in the chicken stock, saffron, and frozen peas; stir to combine and bring the mixture to a boil.
4. Reduce the heat to low and simmer, covered, until the rice is tender and the liquid is absorbed, about 25 minutes.
5. Serve the paella hot.

Nutrition information: Per serving: 270 calories, 12g fat, 26g carbohydrates, 16g protein.

84. Paella with Swordfish and Zucchini

This classic Spanish dish uses fragrant saffron, plump swordfish and crunchy zucchini to create a robust yet simple flavor. Paella with swordfish and zucchini is a hearty meal that can be enjoyed for any occasion.
Serving: Serves 4
Preparation Time: 25 minutes
Ready Time: 50 minutes

Ingredients:
- 2 tablespoons extra-virgin olive oil
- 2 garlic cloves, chopped
- 1 onion, chopped
- 2 teaspoons paprika
- 2 cups short-grain rice
- 2 cups fish or vegetable broth
- 3 cups zucchini, chopped
- 1 teaspoon saffron threads
- 8 ounces swordfish, cubed
- 1 red bell pepper, diced
- Juice of 1 lemon
- Salt, to taste
- Fresh parsley, for garnish

Instructions:
1. Heat the olive oil in a large skillet over medium heat.
2. Add the garlic and onion and cook for about 5 minutes, stirring occasionally, until the onion is softened.
3. Add the paprika and rice and cook for another minute, stirring to combine.
4. Slowly add the broth a little at a time and stir to combine.
5. Add the zucchini, saffron, swordfish, bell pepper and lemon juice and season with salt, to taste.

6. Reduce the heat to low, cover and cook for about 25 minutes, stirring occasionally, until the rice is cooked and the liquid has been absorbed.
7. Garnish with fresh parsley, if desired.

Nutrition information: Calorie 300, Total Fat 7 g, Protein 20 g, Sodium 500 mg, Carbohydrates 41 g

85. Paella with Rabbit and Bell Peppers

Nothing quite beats a traditional Paella, sizzling away with perfectly cooked rice and succulent meats. This recipe for Paella with Rabbit and Bell Peppers is the perfect combination of savory Ingredients and bold flavors that make it a true classic that will have your taste buds singing.
Serving: 6-8
Preparation time: 15 minutes
Ready time: 45 minutes

Ingredients:
- 2 tablespoons olive oil
- 1 large onion, diced
- 2 cloves garlic, minced
- 2 cups white rice
- 1/4 teaspoon saffron threads
- 2 cups vegetable broth
- 1/2 cup wine
- 1/2 teaspoon smoked paprika
- 1 sprig rosemary
- 1 teaspoon sea salt
- 4 bell peppers, diced
- 2 cups cooked rabbit meat, shredded

Instructions:
1. Heat the olive oil in a large sauté pan over medium-high heat.
2. Add the diced onion and garlic and cook until softened, about 5 minutes.
3. Add the white rice and saffron threads and stir to combine.
4. Pour the vegetable broth, wine, smoked paprika, rosemary, and salt into the pan. Bring to a boil.

5. Add the diced bell peppers and the shredded rabbit meat. Simmer for 20 minutes, stirring occasionally.
6. Turn off the heat, cover the pot, and let it sit for 10 minutes. Fluff the Paella with Rabbit and Bell Peppers and serve.

Nutrition information:
Calories: 332, Fat: 9g, Saturated Fat: 2g, Cholesterol: 28mg, Sodium: 575mg, Carbohydrates: 41g, Fiber: 3g, Sugar: 4g, Protein: 13g

86. Paella with Shrimp and Bell Peppers

Paella with Shrimp and Bell Peppers is a delicious Mediterranean dish made with rice, succulent shrimp, red bell peppers, and a variety of savory spices. Serve for a special occasion or a weeknight supper.
Serving: 6
Preparation time: 15 minutes
Ready time: 45 minutes

Ingredients:
- 2 tablespoons olive oil
- 1 large onion, diced
- 2 cloves garlic, minced
- 1 1/2 cup uncooked white rice
- 2 cups vegetable broth
- 2 teaspoons tomato paste
- 1 teaspoon smoked paprika
- 1 teaspoon cumin
- 3 bell peppers, thinly sliced
- 2 pounds large shrimp, shelled and deveined
- 1/2 teaspoon saffron
- 2 tablespoons lemon juice

Instructions:
1. Heat olive oil over medium heat in a large skillet.
2. Add onion and garlic and sauté until fragrant, about 3 minutes.
3. Add rice and toast until lightly golden, about 3 minutes.
4. Stir in the broth, tomato paste, paprika, and cumin.

5. Bring to a simmer, cover and reduce heat to low. Simmer for 15 minutes, or until liquid is absorbed.
6. Uncover the pan and add bell peppers and shrimp. Cook for 5 minutes or until peppers have softened and shrimp are cooked through.
7. Stir in saffron and lemon juice.

Nutrition information: Per Serving: 494 calories; 19.6g fat; 36.8g carbohydrates; 37.4g protein

87. Paella with Crab and Bell Peppers

This paella with succulent crab and bell peppers is an easy to make, satisfying dish that is sure to make your dinner a real hit.
Serving: 4
Preparation time: 10 minutes
Ready time: 40 minutes

Ingredients:
 - 4 ounces white shell crab
 - 2 tablespoons extra virgin olive oil
 - 1 onion, diced
 - 2 bell peppers, diced
 - 2 cloves garlic, minced
 - 2 cups uncooked long-grain white rice
 - 4 cups chicken stock
 - 1 teaspoon paprika
 - 1 teaspoon cayenne pepper
 - 2 tablespoons fresh parsley, minced

Instructions:
1. Heat the olive oil in a Paella pan or large skillet over medium-high heat.
2. Add the onion, bell peppers, and garlic and cook 3-4 minutes or until softened and fragrant.
3. Add the rice and stir to coat the grains with the oil and vegetables.
4. Add the chicken stock, paprika, and cayenne pepper and bring to a boil.
5. Reduce the heat to low and simmer, covered, for 20 minutes.

6. Add the crab and simmer, covered, for an additional 10 minutes or until the crab is cooked through and the rice has absorbed the liquid.

7. Remove from the heat and let sit, covered, for 5 minutes before serving.

8. Garnish with fresh parsley before serving.

Nutrition information: Nutritional values (per serving) – Calories: 326, Total Fat: 5.5g, Sodium: 233mg, Total Carbohydrates: 50g, Protein: 12g.

88. Paella with Chicken and Bell Peppers

Paella with Chicken and Bell Peppers is a traditional Spanish rice dish. It combines savory chicken, bell peppers, and aromatic spices for a flavorful and filling dish.
Serving: 6
Preparation Time: 15 minutes
Ready Time: 45 minutes

Ingredients:
- 2 tablespoons olive oil
- 2 boneless, skinless chicken breasts, chopped
- 1 onion, chopped
- 2 garlic cloves, minced
- 1 red bell pepper, sliced
- 1 cup long-grain white rice
- 2 cups chicken stock
- 2 teaspoons smoked paprika
- 1 teaspoon cayenne pepper
- 1 teaspoon dried oregano
- 1 teaspoon ground cumin
- 1 teaspoon salt
- 1/2 teaspoon ground black pepper
- 1/4 cup chopped parsley

Instructions:
1. Heat the oil in a large paella pan over medium-high heat. Add the chicken and cook until lightly golden, about 8 minutes.

2. Add the onion, garlic, and bell pepper and cook until softened, about 5 minutes.
3. Add the rice and stir to combine. Pour in the chicken stock.
4. Add the paprika, cayenne pepper, oregano, cumin, salt, and pepper. Stir to combine.
5. Reduce the heat to low, cover, and cook until the rice is tender and the liquid has been absorbed, about 20 minutes.
6. Sprinkle with parsley and serve.

Nutrition information: Servings: 6; Calories: 251; Fat: 8g; Carbs: 24g; Protein: 18g

89. Paella with Lamb and Bell Peppers

This is a delicious, smoky and flavorful paella recipe with lamb, bell peppers, and plenty of spices. It is a popular Spanish dish that is great for lunch or dinner.
Serving: 4 people
Preparation Time: 10 minutes
Ready Time: 40 minutes

Ingredients:
- 1/4 cup olive oil
- 2 cloves garlic, minced
- 2 lbs lamb shoulder, cubed
- 1 Onion, diced
- 2 Bell peppers, chopped
- 2 cups of short-grain rice
- 1 teaspoon smoked paprika
- Pinch of saffron
- 2 cups vegetable broth
- 1 red tomato, diced
- 1 teaspoon salt
- 1/2 teaspoon ground black pepper
- 1/4 cup fresh parsley, finely chopped

Instructions:
1. Heat the olive oil in a large skillet over medium-high heat.

2. Add the garlic, lamb, onion, and bell peppers into the pan and cook for 8 minutes.
3. Add the rice and cook for 1 minute.
4. Add the smoked paprika, saffron, vegetable broth, tomato, salt, and ground black pepper into the pan and stir.
5. Reduce the heat to medium-low and simmer for 25 minutes, stirring occasionally.
6. Remove from heat and stir in the parsley. Serve hot.

Nutrition information:
Calories – 479 kcal, Fat – 22.9 g, Protein – 25.4 g, Carbs – 36.8 g, Fiber – 2.5 g, Sugar – 3.8 g, Sodium – 583 mg

90. Paella with Green Peas and Shrimp

Paella with Green Peas and Shrimp is a traditional rice dish with a flavorful combination of shrimp, green peas and vegetables. The smoky flavor of the paprika and saffron makes it a favorite among seafood lovers.
Serving: 4
Preparation Time: 20 minutes
Ready Time: 30 minutes

Ingredients:
- 2 tablespoons olive oil
- 1 onion, finely chopped
- 2 cloves garlic, chopped
- 2 cups long grain rice
- 4 cups chicken broth
- 1/2 teaspoon paprika
- 1/4 teaspoon saffron threads
- Salt and pepper to taste
- 1/2 cup green peas
- 1/2 pound medium sized shrimp, peeled and deveined

Instructions:
1. Heat the olive oil in a large skillet over medium heat.

2. Add the chopped onion and garlic and cook, stirring frequently, until the onion is softened and just beginning to brown.
3. Add the rice and stir until each grain is coated with the oil.
4. Pour in the chicken broth, paprika, saffron, salt and pepper. Bring to a boil, then reduce the heat to low, cover and cook for 15 minutes.
5. Add the green peas and shrimp and cook for another 5 minutes or until the shrimp is cooked through and the rice is tender.
6. Serve hot.

Nutrition information: Per serving:457 calories; 11.1 g fat; 54 g carbohydrates; 23.2 g protein; 307 mg cholesterol; 1149 mg sodium.

91. Paella with Clams and Chicken

Paella with Clams and Chicken is a traditional Spanish rice dish. It is both flavorful and filling, and makes a great main course.
Serving: 4
Preparation Time: 10 minutes
Ready Time: 45 minutes

Ingredients:
- 1 tablespoon olive oil
- 1/2 onion, diced
- 2 cloves of garlic, minced
- 2 cups uncooked long-grain rice
- 1 teaspoon smoked paprika
- 4 cups chicken stock
- 1 can (14.5 ounces) diced tomatoes
- 1/2 teaspoon saffron threads
- 12 clams, scrubbed
- 2 boneless skinless chicken breasts, cubed
- 1 teaspoon salt
- 1/2 teaspoon freshly ground black pepper
- 1/2 cup frozen peas

Instructions:
1. Heat the olive oil in a large skillet over medium-high heat.

2. Add the onion and garlic and cook until the onion is lightly browned, about 5 minutes.
3. Add the rice and paprika and stir to combine. Cook until the rice is lightly toasted, about 2 minutes.
4. Add the chicken stock, diced tomatoes, and saffron threads and stir to combine.
5. Add the clams and chicken and stir to combine.
6. Reduce the heat to low, cover, and simmer, stirring occasionally, until the rice is cooked and the clams are opened, about 30 minutes.
7. Remove from the heat and season with salt and black pepper. Stir in the frozen peas.
8. Serve warm.

Nutrition information:
Calories: 336 kcal, Carbohydrates: 39 g, Protein: 21 g, Fat: 8 g, Saturated Fat: 1 g, Cholesterol: 43 mg, Sodium: 763 mg, Potassium: 505 mg, Fiber: 2 g, Sugar: 2 g, Vitamin A: 308 IU, Vitamin C: 8 mg, Calcium: 56 mg, Iron: 2 mg

92. Paella with Pork and Bell Peppers

Paella with Pork and Bell Peppers is an easy one-pan dish that is sure to impress! Tender pork and bell peppers are simmered in a flavorful saffron broth and combined with short grain rice and veggies for a meal that is equally delicious and nutritious.
Serving: 8
Preparation Time: 20 minutes
Ready Time: 45 minutes

Ingredients:
-1 tablespoon olive oil
-1 pound pork tenderloin, cubed
-1 red bell pepper, diced
-1 yellow bell pepper, diced
-1 teaspoon smoked paprika
-1 teaspoon garlic powder
-1/2 teaspoon ground cumin
-1/4 teaspoon saffron threads

-1/2 cup dry white wine
-3 cups chicken broth
-1 cup short grain rice
-1/2 cup frozen peas

Instructions:
1. Heat olive oil in a large skillet over medium-high heat. Add pork and bell peppers and sauté until pork is cooked through, about 5 minutes.
2. Add paprika, garlic powder, cumin and saffron and cook another minute.
3. Pour in white wine and stir to combine.
4. Add chicken broth and rice, stir and bring to a boil.
5. Reduce heat to medium-low, cover and cook for 15 minutes.
6. Add in peas, stir and cook until rice is tender, about 10 more minutes.
7. Serve paella with pork and bell peppers with a sprinkle of fresh herbs if desired.

Nutrition information: 170 Calories, 10g Fat, 10g Protein, 8g Carbohydrates, 2g Fiber, 82mg Sodium.

93. Paella with Squid and Bell Peppers

Paella with Squid and Bell Peppers is a traditional Spanish dish that packs a punch of flavor! With just a few simple Ingredients, you can create a delicious and satisfying meal that is sure to please.
Serving: 4-6
Preparation Time: 20 minutes
Ready Time: 40 minutes

Ingredients:
-2 tablespoons olive oil
-1 large onion, diced
-2 cloves garlic, minced
-2 bell peppers, chopped
-1 cup white rice
-4 cups chicken broth
-2 cups squid, chopped
-1 teaspoon smoked paprika

-1 teaspoon salt
-1/2 teaspoon freshly ground black pepper
-1 large tomato, diced

Instructions:
1. In a large pot, heat olive oil over medium heat. Add onions and garlic and sauté for 5 minutes, stirring occasionally.
2. Add bell peppers, rice, and chicken broth. Bring to a boil, then reduce heat to low and cook for 20 minutes.
3. Add squid, smoked paprika, salt, and pepper. Cook for an additional 10 minutes until the squid is tender.
4. Lastly, stir in diced tomato and cook until heated through.
5. Serve the paella and enjoy!

Nutrition information: Calories: 263, Total Fat: 6g, Protein: 16g, Total Carbohydrates: 37g, Fiber: 4.6g, Sodium: 1152mg, Sugar: 3.6g.

94. Paella with Beef and Bell Peppers

Paella with Beef and Bell Peppers is a classic Spanish dish, featuring rich flavors of rice, beef, bell peppers, and spices. It is sure to make for a flavorful meal!
Serving: 4 servings
Preparation Time: 15 minutes
Ready Time: 45 minutes

Ingredients:
- 2 tablespoons of olive oil
- 2 cloves of garlic, minced
- 2 teaspoons of paprika
- 1/2 teaspoon of ground cumin
- Salt and pepper, to taste
- 1/2 cup of dry white wine
- 1/2 cup of chicken stock
- 1 teaspoon of freshly squeezed lemon juice
- 1 cup of long-grain rice
- 1/2 pound of lean ground beef

- 1 red bell pepper, diced
- 1/2 cup of frozen peas
- 1/4 cup of chopped fresh parsley

Instructions:
1. Heat the olive oil in a large pot over medium-high heat.
2. Add the garlic and cook for 2 minutes, stirring occasionally.
3. Add the paprika, cumin, salt, and pepper, and cook for 1 minute longer.
4. Add the white wine, chicken stock, and lemon juice. Stir in the rice, beef, and bell pepper.
5. Reduce heat to low and simmer for 25 minutes, stirring occasionally.
6. Add the frozen peas and simmer for 10 minutes longer, or until the liquid is absorbed.
7. Remove from heat and stir in the parsley. Serve warm.

Nutrition information: Calories: 315, Total Fat: 11g, Cholesterol: 37mg, Sodium: 228mg, Total Carbohydrates: 32g, Protein: 16g

95. Paella with Asparagus and Shrimp

Paella with Asparagus and Shrimp is a delicate dish characterized by a subtle mixture of seafood, vegetables, and aromatics. The combination of shrimp, asparagus and white rice with saffron and garlic creates a colorful and flavorful medley.
Serving: 4
Preparation time: 10 minutes
Ready time: 40 minutes

Ingredients:
- 1/4 cup olive oil
-1/2 cup chopped onion
-2 cloves of minced garlic
-1 cup arborio rice
-3 cups vegetable broth
-1/4 teaspoon saffron threads
-1/2 teaspoon sea salt
-1/4 teaspoon pepper

- 1/2 pound medium shrimp, peeled and deveined
- 1/2 pound asparagus, trimmed and cut into 1-inch pieces
- 1/4 cup chopped fresh parsley

Instructions:
1. Heat the olive oil in a large skillet over medium heat. Add the onion and garlic and sauté until softened, about 5 minutes.
2. Add the rice and stir to combine. Pour in the broth and stir in the saffron, salt, and pepper.
3. Bring the mixture to a boil and then reduce the heat to low. Simmer until the liquid is absorbed and the rice is cooked, about 20 minutes.
4. Meanwhile, add the shrimp and asparagus to a separate skillet and sauté until the shrimp are cooked through, about 4 minutes.
5. Once the rice is done, add in the shrimp mixture and stir to combine.
6. Serve the paella hot, garnished with parsley.

Nutrition information:
Serving size: 1/4 of the recipe
Calories: 310
Total fat: 11g
Cholesterol: 96mg
Sodium: 538mg
Total carbohydrates: 34g
Dietary fiber: 3g
Protein: 14g

96. Paella with Lobster and Shrimp

This recipe for Paella with Lobster and Shrimp combines two seafoods with a blend of vegetables and spices in a flavorful rice dish that is perfect for any occasion.
Serving: 8-10
Preparation Time: 25 minutes
Ready Time: 1 hour 25 minutes

Ingredients:
- 2 tablespoons olive oil
- 2 small yellow onions, peeled and diced

- 2 cloves garlic, minced
- 1 red bell pepper, seeded and diced
- 1 green bell pepper, seeded and diced
- 2 chorizo sausage links, diced or crumbled
- 1 teaspoon ground turmeric
- 1 teaspoon paprika
- 1 teaspoon ground cumin
- 2 cups Valencia-style rice
- 4 cups chicken stock
- 1 14 ounce can diced tomatoes, drained
- 2 cups frozen peas
- 1 cooked lobster, cut into 1-inch pieces
- 2 cups cooked shrimp
- 1 cup fresh parsley, chopped
- Salt and pepper to taste

Instructions:
1. Heat the olive oil in a large skillet or paella pan over medium heat until shimmering.
2. Add the onions and cook until softened, about 4 minutes.
3. Add the garlic and bell peppers and cook for an additional 4 minutes.
4. Add the chorizo and cook for 3 minutes.
5. Add the turmeric, paprika, and cumin, and cook for 1 minute.
6. Add the rice and stir to coat with the spices and vegetables.
7. Add the chicken stock and diced tomatoes and bring to a simmer.
8. Reduce heat to low and simmer for 20 minutes, stirring occasionally.
9. Add the frozen peas, lobster, shrimp, parsley, and salt and pepper, and stir to combine.
10. Simmer for an additional 10 minutes, or until the rice is tender and the liquid has been absorbed.

Nutrition information: Per serving: 370 Calories; 10g Fat; 83mg Cholesterol; 617mg Sodium; 33g Carbohydrates; 4g Fiber; 19g Sugar; 18g Protein.

97. Paella with Sausage and Shrimp

Paella with Sausage and Shrimp is a classic Spanish dish that combines flavorful sausages, juicy shrimp, and fresh vegetables cooked in a flavorful rice dish. This version is sure to be a crowd pleaser and a delight to serve during a Spanish-themed meal!

Serving: 4
Preparation time: 10 minutes
Ready time: 40 minutes

Ingredients:
- 1 tablespoon olive oil
- 4 fresh sausages, cut into pieces
- 1 onion, diced
- 2 cloves of garlic, minced
- 2 cups uncooked short grain rice
- 2 large ripe tomatoes, diced
- 4 cups chicken broth
- 1 teaspoon saffron threads
- Pinch of salt
- 1 cup cooked shrimp
- 2 tablespoons parsley, chopped

Instructions:

1. Heat the olive oil in a large skillet over medium heat. Add the sausage pieces and cook for about 5 minutes, or until lightly golden brown.
2. Add the onion and garlic to the pan, stir to coat with the oil. Cook for about 5 minutes, or until the onion is softened.
3. Stir in the uncooked rice, tomatoes, chicken broth, saffron threads, and a pinch of salt to the skillet. Increase the heat to high and bring to a boil.
4. Reduce the heat to low, cover and simmer for 20 minutes, or until all the liquid is absorbed and the rice is cooked.
5. Gently stir in the cooked shrimp and parsley. Simmer for an additional 5 minutes.
6. Serve paella with sausage and shrimp hot.

Nutrition information: per serving, 6 net carbs, 15 g protein, 15 g fat, 260 calories.

98. Paella with Cod and Shrimp

Delicious and flavorful, this paella with cod and shrimp is the perfect meal for any occasion. Serve it among family and friends for a truly special dinner.

Serving: 6
Preparation Time: 30 minutes
Ready Time: 1 hour

Ingredients:
- 2 tablespoons olive oil
- 2/3 cup paella rice
- 1 onion, chopped
- 2 cloves garlic, minced
- 1/2 teaspoon smoked paprika
- 3 cups chicken broth
- 1 red bell pepper, chopped
- 1 green bell pepper, chopped
- 1 teaspoon saffron
- 1/2 teaspoon salt
- 12 ounces cod, cut into 1-inch pieces
- 12 ounces shrimp, cooked
- 2 tablespoons frozen peas
- 2 tablespoons chopped fresh parsley

Instructions:
1. Heat oil in a paella pan or large skillet over medium-high heat.
2. Add rice and onion and cook, stirring frequently, until onion is softened, 5-6 minutes.
3. Add garlic and paprika, and cook, stirring constantly, for 2 minutes.
4. Add chicken broth, bell peppers, saffron, and salt, and bring to a boil.
5. Reduce heat to low and simmer, uncovered, for 15 minutes.
6. Add cod and shrimp and simmer, uncovered, for an additional 10 minutes.
7. Add peas and cook for 2 minutes more.
8. Sprinkle paella with parsley and serve warm.

Nutrition information: (Per Serving)
Calories: 203
Fat: 8 g

Saturated Fat: 1 g
Cholesterol: 120 mg
Sodium: 1080 mg
Carbohydrates: 11 g
Fiber: 1 g
Protein: 16 g

99. Paella with Pork and Shrimp

This classic Spanish one-pan dish features a flavorful mixture of pork, shrimp, and a mix of colorful vegetables and spices in a gloriously saffron-scented paella rice. Serve this flavorful paella dish for a delightful dinner.
Serving: 8 servings
Preparation Time: 30 minutes
Ready Time: 1 hour and 15 minutes

Ingredients:
- 4 teaspoons olive oil
- 1 pound pork shoulder, cut into cubes
- Salt and freshly cracked black pepper, to taste
- 1 onion, diced
- 2 cloves garlic, minced
- 2 red bell peppers, diced
- 1 teaspoon smoked paprika
- 1 (14.5-ounce) can diced tomatoes
- 1 teaspoon saffron threads
- 2 cups paella rice
- 1/2 teaspoon dried oregano
- 4 cups chicken broth
- 8 ounces cooked shrimp

Instructions:
1. Heat the oil in a large paella pan over medium-high heat. Add the pork cubes and season with salt and pepper. Cook for 8-10 minutes, stirring frequently, until browned.
2. Add the onion, garlic, and bell pepper to the pan and cook for 3-4 minutes, until softened.

3. Stir in the paprika, tomatoes, saffron, rice, oregano and chicken broth. Bring the mixture to a boil, then reduce the heat to low. Cover and simmer for 15 minutes.

4. Add the shrimp to the pan and stir to combine. Cover and simmer for an additional 5 minutes, or until the rice is tender and the shrimp is cooked through.

5. Serve hot.

Nutrition information: Calories: 388, Protein: 22g, Fat: 14g, Carbohydrates: 36g, Fiber: 2g, Sugar: 5g, Sodium: 765mg

CONCLUSION

The Paella Master: 99 Authentic Recipes for the Classic Spanish Dish is a must-have cookbook for anyone looking to learn how to master the classic Spanish dish, as well as for the experienced home cook. It provides clear step-by-step instructions on how to craft the perfect paella with delicious, authentic flavors. The book also covers the history of the iconic dish and provides a huge variety of delicious recipes including a range of traditional and modern options. It is packed full of detailed illustrations, tips and advice, and paeleera collections – all essential to help the reader create the perfect feast. In sum, The Paella Master: 99 Authentic Recipes for the Classic Spanish Dish is an essential cookbook for those looking to perfect their paella, as well as for the novice cook who is just getting started. With its wide range of recipes, detailed instructions and advice, and beautiful illustrations, this cookbook will help anyone create a delicious and memorable paella. The Paella Master will keep readers coming back time and again to create a variety of unique dishes that are both easy to make and full of flavor. With this cookbook, you'll be able to serve up an amazing paella every time!

Milton Keynes UK
Ingram Content Group UK Ltd.
UKHW032028181124
2932UKWH00011B/601